BRAM E GIEBEN

THE DARKEST TIMELINE

Living in a World with No Future

THE DARKEST TIMELINE
Bram E. Gieben

First published by Revol Press 2024

Revol Press, Oulu, Finland / Raleigh, United States

First edition

Text copyright: Bram E. Gieben 2024

Print ISBN: 978-952-94-9035-6
ebook ISBN: 978-952-94-9036-3

Design: Valtteri Harakka

CONTENTS

Domination over nature necessarily entails the class domination of people over other people... The way to rid ourselves of our masters is not for humankind to become a collective master over nature, but to recognise the imposture in the very notion of the Master.

—Slavoj Žižek
Living in the End Times

GENERATION TICK-TOCK

> To the often-heard question "Who are they, this new generation?" one is tempted to answer, "Those who hear the ticking." And to the other question, "Who are they who utterly deny them?" the answer may well be, "Those who do not know, or refuse to face, things as they really are."[1]
>
> —Hannah Arendt
> *On Violence*

What does it mean to live in a world with no future? In 2024, techno-optimist hopes for space travel, transhumanism and the "singularity" collide with the realities of climate collapse, democratic decline, widespread conflict, political disinformation and algorithmic distortion. How do we imagine a way through these challenges? How do we navigate a discourse about the future laden with ideology, propaganda, spectacle, and unrealistic utopianism? How do we squarely face the idea of societal collapse in a responsible and measured way, when apocalyptic scenes dominate our imaginations? For years, in lieu of answers, I lost myself in disaster fiction. Now, I believe we must explore our dystopian present.

---

1   Hannah Arendt, *On Violence* (Harvest Books / Houghton Mifflin Harcourt, 1970), p18.

Alan Moore's 1986 graphic novel *Watchmen*[2] begins with the tick of the so-called Doomsday Clock. Maintained since 1947 by members of the board who publish the *Bulletin of the Atomic Scientists*, a group set up by Albert Einstein and others in the wake of the Second World War and the bombing of Nagasaki, the time displayed on the clock is an indicator of how close the world is to nuclear holocaust. Hannah Arendt would have been aware of the ticking of the Doomsday Clock by the time she wrote the passage above in 1963. Despite her scepticism over their tactics, she gave a small concession to the doom-fixated radicals of the 60s. They were the first generation to have to live with the existential threat of a nuclear holocaust. Before the Cold War concept of "mutually assured destruction" entered the popular imagination in the wake of the Nagasaki blast, and the revelation of the horrors of the Nazi holocaust, the possibility of humanity's complete erasure and extinction was one few contemplated seriously in anything but abstract or religious terms.

My generation are the children of the 60s and 70s radicals Arendt criticised in *On Violence*. Our parents learned to live with Cold War bomb drills, we learned of the horror of atomic warfare from terrifying TV shows such as 1984's *Threads*. We also learned to live with the emerging threat of climate collapse. After the fall of the Berlin Wall in 1989 and the end of the USSR, both the possibility of nuclear annihilation and the prospect of some future climate catastrophe would come to be seen as somehow tempered by the victorious paradigm of neoliberal democracy and economics, embodied in steady technological and scientific progress. Francis Fukuyama's comforting 1992 prediction that

---

2   Alan Moore, Dave Gibbons and John Higgins, *Watchmen* (DC Comics, 1986-1987).

liberal democracy would become the global norm became a pillar of government policy in the UK and US. The Doomsday Clock was set back to seventeen minutes to midnight in the early 1990s following the success of international nuclear non-proliferation treaties. In the decades since, it has swung towards twelve again, and now stands at 90 seconds from oblivion, the closest it has ever been to midnight.

Today, such a cacophony of disaster vies for our attention that it drowns out even the ticking of the clock. Perhaps it is easier today to speak of a roar; a blood-dimmed tide that can be sensed or felt, just out of earshot, in the near distance. This current generation are not "those who hear the ticking." We are those for whom the ticking is drowned out by that roar; those so close to the final tick that we can already sense screams and suffering. We often wonder whether the tick counts not how much time we have left, but how late we already are. We are no more or less prone to catastrophism or naivety than the generations that have preceded us, but we are informed about the chaos of the world, as no generation before us has ever been.

In these essays, I set out to explore the aesthetics, ideologies, technologies and dangers that shape how we think about our possible futures, or lack of them. In "Zero Future," I offer an analysis of the escapist aesthetics of apocalypse fiction, the truths inherent in cyberpunk, and the comforting beliefs of Baby Boomer space pioneers. In "Transhuman Nostalgia," I argue that if our world is burning, we cannot retreat to the future via a "post-human" singularity, because our technologies share our vulnerabilities, our flaws, and our psychopathologies.

In "Cascading Catastrophic Colony Collapse" I draw on recent scientific studies into climate-caused societal collapse, and the fragility of our political, economic, and cultural systems. I attempt to answer questions over why we should survive as a species, and what a future beyond collapse might look like for those that endure. "Meme War" offers a re-appreciation of John Barnes' neglected 1995 cult cyberpunk novel *Kaleidoscope Century*, with its prescient analysis of human-technological confluence, biowar and collapsing democracy. "Game of Drones" looks at the coming confluence of drone technology, artificial intelligence and the total surveillance of the "Digital Panopticon." I explore the enduring power of Nick Bostrom's "Simulation Argument" paper, and its representation in culture through films like *The Matrix*.

In "Type Zero Kardashev" I contrast two well-known thought experiments about our cosmic existence, as Kardashev's theory of interstellar species development goes up against Fermi's pessimistic paradox. I look at the phenomenon of the online game *Randonautica*, and what it might tell us about consensus reality. In "Infinite Verse," I explore the vast fictional shared realities of the space simulators *No Man's Sky* and *Eve Online*, to see if they have lessons to teach us about the meaningful ways we can occupy virtual space, and the dangers inherent in letting it be colonised, monetised and owned by a selfish billionaire class.

"Liminal City of the Spotless Brand" offers a trip inside the "backrooms," the forgotten no-places that exist in the interstices between the bland corporate pseudo-realities of our brand-choked inner cities. Finally, in "Pandora Dynamics," I look at the tradition of prophecy itself, from the Greek myths of Pandora and Cassandra to so-called "scientific" prediction systems such as effective altruism, longtermism and Cliodynamics.

I have long been captivated by the dilemma posed by Mark Fisher in 2009's *Capitalist Realism*.[3] How do we imagine ourselves out of, not just the end of the world, but the end of capitalism? I believe we must begin with a full and frank engagement with the worst case scenarios that could proceed from our precarious present. At such historical moments of the greatest threat and possibility, we cannot give in to absolute pessimism. In the TV show *Community*, the Darkest Timeline begins with the roll of a dice, a moment of chance and significance that leads to chaos and destruction. We face such a moment now. We need a paradigm shift that changes how we look at culture, technology, ideology and society. To achieve that, we must look without flinching at the confluence of threats we now face. To confront the possibility that we have no future is also to demand that the future be reimagined anew.

—Bram E. Gieben, Glasgow, 2024

---

3   Mark Fisher, *Capitalist Realism: Is There No Alternative?* (Zer0 Books, 2009).

one

ZERO FUTURE

> The future is already here — it's just not evenly distributed.[1]
>
> —Attributed to William Gibson

Imaginationland is an episode of the adult animation *South Park* which revolves around a character who becomes ruler of a fantasy realm where all fictional characters are real and stories are "true". It echoes Alan Moore's concept of "ideaspace" — where all human conceptual and linguistic knowledge is stored in a "space" similar to the collective unconscious. The territory of the apocalypse is not just an overpopulated region of Imaginationland. It is also an aesthetic that proclaims both its own incipiency and its latency in culture. The endtimes aesthetic is with us in the present. If it is easier to imagine the end of the world than the end of capitalism, then it certainly seems as if there is a lot of profit to be derived from the simpler cognitive challenge.

From the near-future resource conflict anxiety of the original *Mad Max* to the crumbling, autocratic dystopia of *Children of*

---

1   William Gibson was quoted as saying this in The Economist, in 2003. Since then, his original utterance of the phrase has been a matter of some debate, even by Gibson himself. He says the idea would have been something he spoke about often with friends in the 80s and 90s, rather than being the decisive statement (and often-cited mantra) it has become. An interesting deep dive into the origins of the phrase can be read at: https://quoteinvestigator.com/2012/01/24/future-has-arrived (Accessed Feb. 15, 2024).

Men, the imagery and aesthetic of the apocalypse is so commodified that it has ceased to function as a dire, prescient warning. We have become the apocalypse narrative. The story tropes and visual aesthetics of both societal collapse and the post-apocalypse that follows are so embedded that they serve as memetic joke-fodder in *Rick and Morty*, or the backdrop to teen romance and frustrated hormones in *The Hunger Games* and its myriad clones and imitators (being itself an iteration of Koushun Takami's novel *Battle Royale*, and its subsequent film adaptation directed by Kinji Fukasaku).[2] No matter how played out, no matter how over-analyzed and emptied of all symbolic power, narratives of the post-apocalypse remain latent in our culture and media, because in the past they have proven prescient. There's a crushing inevitability to the refugee camps in *Children of Men* that now find their visual echoes wherever there is a tent city, from Skid Row in Los Angeles to Calais in France; from the the camps at Um Shalaya and Mukjar in Darfur to huddled migrants on the border between Belarus and Poland. In the decade and a half since the film of *Children of Men* was released (three decades on from P.D. James' original novel)[3] its imagery has acquired the charge of documentary footage.

The relevance of the apocalyptic imagery we have culturally reveled in for the past few decades will become increasingly apparent as the unavoidable effects of catastrophic climate collapse continue to unfold. 2015's *Mad Max: Fury Road* was a long way from the kitchen-sink amphetamine realism of George Miller's original, but the director's anticipation of an Australia leeched completely dry of water and energy sources, descending back into ruthlessly Darwinian resource conflict is perhaps closer than we

---

2   Koushun Takami, trans. Yuji Oniki, *Battle Royale* (Viz Media, 2003).

3   P.D. James, *The Children of Men* (Faber and Faber, 1992).

think. The aestheticized apocalypse of *Fury Road* is a comfortable fantasy compared to the sense of tumbling, unavoidable collapse that haunted the original, because the pre-collapse dystopia of *Mad Max* is closer to our own time, our own reality.

The Japanese author Haruki Murakami wrote: "Everyone, deep in their hearts, is waiting for the end of the world to come."[4] Whether this is a modern phenomenon or an ageless one is a valid question, but the imminent threat of climate collapse makes nonsense of any notion that this generation, or those that follow it, might consider the apocalypse completely in the abstract, or through a spiritual or metaphorical lens. The reality is that we or our children will in all likelihood have to watch a lot of people die, whether through extreme climate events, resource depletion, supply chain failure, or conflict precipitated by mass migration in the wake of rising sea levels and temperatures. For everyone alive now, the question of the survival of human society and the likely survival of the majority of other animals now living on the planet is an existential one.

Perhaps these very real, extinction-level questions posed by the threat of human-caused climate change are poorly understood through the vector of apocalypse aesthetics. Our experiences of modernity, of the future, of collapse and lack and impoverishment are wildly asymmetrical. The great sociologist and political theorist Stuart Hall wrote in 1988:

---

4   The novel that this is taken from, *Hard-Boiled Wonderland and The End of the World* (Kodansha International, 1985), is Murakami's most disturbing and visionary work. In his Kafka-esque proto-cyberpunk fantasy, "The End of the World" is a place — a town surrounded by high walls with its own social codes and norms.

> Modernity has acquired a relentlessly uneven and contradictory character: material abundance here, producing poverty and immiseration there; greater diversity and choice — but often at the cost of commodification, fragmentation and isolation. More opportunities for participation — but only at the expense of subordinating oneself to the laws of the market. Novelty and innovation — but driven by what often appear to be false needs. The rich "West" — and the famine stricken South. Forms of "development" which destroy faster than they create. The city... transformed into the anonymous city, the sprawling city, the inner city, the abandoned city.[5]

Nothing in our current world is "evenly distributed". This applies to politics and economics as much as it does to science. The aspects of the cyberpunk genre that deal with economic inequality, the corporate capture of state apparatus and the cultural pressure that rapid technological advances apply to social worlds remain some of the most useful fictional tools we have for understanding the present. The 2008 Mexican cyberpunk film *Sleep Dealer*, directed by Alex Rivera, depicts a world of closed borders that nonetheless relies on an expendable, exploitable working class of foreign labor. Rather than cross borders to seek a better life, the citizens of Rivera's future Mexico work in virtual reality, in gigantic battery farm-like factories. Their haptic rigs control robots on distant construction sites in the developed

---

5   Stuart Hall, "The Meaning of New Times," re-published in *Selected Political Writings*, ed. Sally Davison, David Featherstone, Michael Rustin and Bill Schwarz (Duke University Press, 2017), p256.

world. They often work punishing twenty-hour shifts. Sometimes the loss of self experienced by these workers, as they act through the robots, causes the machine to have an accident. When this happens, workers can die in real life — hence the name given to the factories, the "sleep dealers" of the title.

Along with some prescient commentary on drone technology, resource scarcity and the leveraging of confession stories on social media, the film's central premise vividly illustrates the way in which technological progress does not necessarily imply the liberation of the working class through automation. It depicts a far more plausible scenario — that technological innovation will produce new forms of class domination and exploitation in pursuit of ever-greater profit. This is not a vision of the apocalypse, it is a metaphor for our current situation. Just as William Gibson's novels have crept closer to the current historical moment, the genre of cyberpunk has kept pace, so that the near-future of our dystopias has become the near-present. The aesthetic of the post-apocalypse is now just a fantasy, no matter how bleak. Collapse fantasies express the desire to escape from a dystopian present to an exoticized apocalypse, usually with vastly simpler stakes. They are about good versus evil, or humankind versus nature.

Our obsession with the abstract or symbolic representation of apocalypse and collapse as a truth-event in some imagined future signals our inability to see that many people now live in realities that are in every way concurrent with the experiences we see represented as "post-apocalyptic." As the artist Anjalika Sagar explains:

> When does the apocalypse begin? For people who were kidnapped and thrown into slavery, the apocalypse began then; when forms of deforestation started

in the Amazon of the Indigenous people the apocalypse might have started then. There are many times
in which we might enter the apocalypse.[6]

The revolutionary message that too few apocalypse movies or stories convey is that the apocalypse has already happened — that
it is happening to billions of people, right now as you read this.
To embrace one's own radical powerlessness in the face of such
unpredictable existential threats is to live in a constant state of
hypervigilance, attuned only to the present moment, and the goal
of survival. This is the message of Rivera's *Sleep Dealer*. The best
cyberpunk offers a pragmatic way to conceptualize our future(s),
or the lack of one, as one of the protagonists of Gibson's novel
Pattern Recognition explains:

> We have no idea, now, of who or what the inhabitants
> of our future might be. In that sense, we have no future.
> Not in the sense that our grandparents had a future, or
> thought they did. Fully imagined cultural futures were
> the luxury of another day, one in which "now" was of
> some greater duration. For us, of course, things can
> change so abruptly, so violently, so profoundly, that
> futures like our grandparents' have insufficient "now"

---

6   Anjalika Sagar, quoted by Oliver Basciano, "When We Grew up,
     Luis Buñuel was on Channel 4: The Proudly Highbrow Otolith
     Group," *The Guardian*, Jul. 6, 2022, https://www.theguardian.com/
     artanddesign/2022/jul/06/luis-bunuel-channel-4-proudly-highbrow-oto-
     lith-group-apocalypse (Accessed Feb. 4, 2024).

to stand on. We have no future because our present is
too volatile...[7]

The future used to look different. In 1977, US President
Jimmy Carter watched as the Voyager probe was launched on its
long journey towards and through the outer reaches of our solar
system, and eventually out into interstellar space. Inscribed on the
probe was a message from the President: "We are attempting to
survive our time so we may live into yours." Such a message can
only be seen as the product of a deep and ingrained optimism,
borne of the absolute conviction that a future would arrive for
us to "live into." In the asymmetrical post-apocalyptic society we
inhabit today, such a future is in reality radically unthinkable, yet
we nonetheless still fervently, naively anticipate it. Carter's words
are just empty symbols, scratched into a tin can that will in all
probability drift through space until it burns up in the atmosphere
of some unknown gas giant, vast distances from our choking
planet as we murder each other over scraps of food.

Carter's message was one of hope, and of anticipated triumph. It shows that his generation believed that the struggles
and enmity of the Cold War era would be overcome by the ghost
of progress, uniting humanity in a system that would transcend
politics and unite us under one triumphant banner. This was
the post-capitalist future imagined in the original 1960s series
of *Star Trek*. Out beyond the stars, beyond the reach of history
and money and politics, *homo utopiana* would be free to shag its
way through beautiful alien populations of othered "natives" —
always looking for the undiscovered place, the unseen sight. It's
a space-age colonial fantasy, and only makes sense if imagined

---

7   William Gibson, *Pattern Recognition* (Penguin, 2003), p57.

as Federation propaganda. The British Empire also told itself its mission was to civilize and improve. The Star Trek "mirror universe," in which the Federation is a bastion of galactic fascism, is probably a more realistic depiction of what it would take to put humanity among the stars.

It begs the question, why would we leave Earth? We care less and less to see the lives that play out beyond our reach, in other places. What would we truly wish to know of the suffering of alien species on distant worlds? We know very little of the suffering or experiences of those beyond the arbitrary borders of our own cities, countries and continents. Where would such unity, the will to somehow escape Earth come from? This, too, is radically unthinkable in the context of the unequal, uneven human culture we have created. The evidence shows that we do not truly care about other people — or rather, people we have "othered." We will always be content to watch them burn or drown on television, as long as the fences around our little compounds remain staunch. Perhaps that is simply one of the deepest human instincts, the preference for one's own "tribe," however that is defined. Such instincts are easily weaponized. The idea that we are powerless to be anything other than detached spectators is also a self-fulfilling prophecy.

"We don't deserve to be triumphant because we are wholly complicit with the system we despise,"[8] writes the critic and philosopher Mike Watson. Visions of apocalypse are nothing but an idiot's fantastical escape from the realities of this complicity. Wandering in the fallen worlds of our televisual, cinematic and video game dream-sleep, we play the part of the survivor, the oppressed, the rebel and the revolutionary; sometimes even the savior. Dreams of apocalypse are more often than not dreams of

---

8   Mike Watson, *The Memeing of Mark Fisher* (Zero Books, 2021), p59.

redemption, and nostalgic retrieval. As such, they are not even useful works of fantasy.

What can be said about a culture whose escapist fantasies are as drab, bleak and brutalist as the washed-out tones of Denis Villeneuve films such as *Arrival, Dune,* or *Blade Runner 2049*? The beauty within is numb, leeched of color, aestheticized to the point of anesthesia. In Villeneuve's futures, there is nothing to be dreamed of or desired. Just bleak, inhuman architecture, populated by ghosts — much like the ruins an extinct humanity will leave behind. It can sometimes feel as if even depicting this haunted mythscape is a capitulation to its inevitability. As the journalist Laurie Penny writes:

> Capitalism cannot imagine a future beyond itself that isn't utter butchery. This is because late capitalism has always been a death cult. The tiny-minded incompetents in charge cannot handle a problem that can't be fixed simply by sacrificing poor, vulnerable, and otherwise expendable individuals.[9]

The fully imagined cultural futures Gibson views as impossible for us to now grasp are the product of a radically atemporal cultural moment. All historical eras, but in particular the vivid, imagistic, mediated truth-events of twentieth-century history and aesthetics appear superimposed over each other, taking place simultaneously. This represents the total commodification of history, making the present also radically unthinkable, just as

9   Laurie Penny, "This Is Not the Apocalypse You Were Looking For," *Wired*, Mar. 30, 2020, https://www.wired.com/story/coronavirus-apocalypse-myths (Accessed Feb. 4, 2024).

Mark Fisher described any alternative to capitalism. Any New Thing created in our culture is inherently designed to prefigure the aesthetic of its own nostalgia, which will, in any case, be a complex composite of preexisting nostalgia aesthetics, leading to impossible designations, such as "Retro Future." We're at peak remake, trapped in the prequel problem — our fates already known and assured, replete with false promises and choices which lead nowhere. We're at the event horizon of cultural singularity, beyond which there is only collapse, and forgetting. As such, we are free to enjoy comfortable dystopias. There are many to choose from. The revolutionary potential that remains in cyberpunk, inherent in all great science fiction, resides in its description of the point we occupy *in the present*. Science fiction is not just escapism or prophecy, it is the literature of those dispossessed from the present and alienated by the future. The only true possible future is already here. We currently occupy that far point beyond which the future cannot be imagined. Cyberpunk is now. There is nothing after.

two

TRANSHUMAN NOSTALGIA

The past is fucking prologue.[1]

—Roger Stone

Machiavellian political consultant Roger Stone's political "rules" and the "12 Rules for Life" set out by conservative self-help salesman Jordan Peterson have a similar tenor. They both betray a knowing surety that while nostalgia should always guide the choices and norms of the world, it should be a nostalgia that suits only the protagonist of what Joseph Campbell called the "hero's journey."[2] For the Petersonian hero, the past is surely a prologue. It all leads up to the moment of departure, the epic quest, and the triumphant return. Just as Stone's adage (taken from a book simply called *Stone's Rules*[3]) points to the ease with which political fortunes can be turned around, and past mistakes erased, Peterson's mythos asks us to consider only one viewpoint on the world: our own. Their philosophies are both born of a ruthless social Darwinism that privileges the idea of autocratic,

---

1   Roger Stone, quoted by Michael Kruse, "Roger Stone's Last Dirty Trick", *Politico*, Jan. 25, 2019, https://www.politico.com/magazine/story/2019/01/25/roger-stone-last-dirty-trick-224217 (Accessed Feb. 4, 2024).

2   The 'hero's journey' or monomyth concept was popularised in Joseph Campbell's influential book *The Hero with A Thousand Faces* (Pantheon Books, 1949).

3   Roger Stone, *Stone's Rules - How to Win at Politics, Business, and Style* (Skyshore Publishing, 2018).

great (male) figures. This is a basic misunderstanding of the cosmology of the ancient myths upon which Campbell theorized the archetypal "hero's journey" was based. The mythic hero is not destined to break the chains of the past and re-configure the future through sheer force of will. Rather, he is a pawn of fate; a plaything of indifferent or capricious gods. The hero is a straw man, and the past is a settled fact. Prologues have weight, they fix the shape of the drama to come.

Why are stories important? This is a vital question in the current political and cultural landscape, as long overdue conversations about identity and representation begin to emerge from the political fringes (though not for the first time). This is a moment where historical narratives, our collective prologues, feel open to question. There is a revolutionary potential in movements like MeToo and Black Lives Matter that could reckon with the kinds of wildly inaccurate myth-telling our capitalist societies have indulged in for centuries. From narratives about the slave trade and the institutions it funded, to real engagement with the racial, gender, and class dynamics of policing and imprisonment, the need to interrogate our prologues has never been more urgent.

The fact this makes many people uncomfortable is understandable. Adam Curtis, the documentary filmmaker, has often explored the distance between cultural and historical truth in his work. In a 2021 interview, he speculated that the future "might be a moment when all the old stories that made sense of the world are collapsing," asking whether the experiencing self might become privileged over collective narrative.[4] Curtis, a liberal in the classical

---

4   Charlie Brooker, "In Conversation with Adam Curtis," *Vice Magazine*, Feb. 11, 2021, https://www.vice.com/en/article/4ad8db/adam-curtis-charlie-brooker-cant-get-you-out-of-my-head (Accessed Feb. 4, 2024).

sense, seems to see a historical present where the questioning of imperial, colonial and capitalist narratives has created a vacuum. His conclusions are far from comforting. He continues:

> … and then from somewhere that we can't possibly imagine at the moment, someone will start to reassemble all those fragments in a completely new way — and out of that will come the new big story. That actually we might be living through a moment of almost complete freedom from meaning, which is why we are so terrified and anxious. It might be like that moment in the eye of a storm. Outside, the giant forces of history roar on — but in the eye it has gone quiet and we are just experiencing, but have no story to tell each other.

There remain very few coherent narratives on the left or mainstream of politics that can reassemble the fragments of history in a new way. The left has plenty of expertise in the fields of deconstruction, disruption, and networked protest. It encompasses many sophisticated community and volunteer networks tied to political activism, which have evolved to do what they see as necessary to mitigate the worsening disaster effects of apocalypse capitalism. The academic left, and its media, can deconstruct the "old big story" of capitalism in a million ways, but it nonetheless feels like the only "new big stories" are the empty promises of authoritarian populists and the crazy propagandistic conspiracy theories they sustain. This is what gives the current moment a particularly apocalyptic hue.

In moments of paralysis and decline, fear controls the narrative. As the cultural critic Henry A. Giroux writes: "History as an act of dangerous memory is whitewashed, purged of utopian ideals and replaced by apocalyptic fantasies. These include narratives of decline, fear, insecurity, anxiety and visions of imminent danger, often expressed in the language of invasion, dangerous hordes, criminal and disease-infected others."[5] The "dangerous memory" of nostalgia-powered corporate capitalism is that it has always been thus, that there can be no alternative.

Apocalyptic visions underline the ideological position that deviation from capitalism would be too dangerous. The genuine left, or even the truly liberal center, have not held meaningful power in capitalism's wealthiest nations for a long time, and so they struggle to dictate any counter-narrative beyond mitigation. The efforts of those engaged in professional left or liberal politics are too often diverted into projects that are reformist, and like politicians of all stripes, they too can be (and too often are) careerists and power-hungry parasites. Those engaged in revolutionary or community politics do what they can, but they are easily dismissed by state propaganda or repression; or in the case of infrastructure activists, co-opted by it through systems of grants, loans, and petty bureaucracy.

The powerful narratives of the right may be lies, and they may be horrific, but they offer a coherence to the false nostalgia that co-opts the capitalist imaginary. Conservative myths promise to return to the time when "capitalism worked" and everyone had a "fair share" of opportunity. This false meritocracy is the utopia

---

5 Henry A. Giroux, "Depoliticisation is a Deadly Weapon of Neoliberal Fascism," *Truthout*, Oct. 15, 2019, https://truthout.org/articles/depoliticization-is-a-deadly-weapon-of-neoliberal-fascism (Accessed Feb. 4, 2024).

of capitalist realism, at both ends of the political spectrum. The "change" promised by generous and humane activism is an illusion of collective faith. The "change" promised by right-wing demagogues is one of violent negation — an image of catharsis, restorative justice; even revenge. This is nominally undertaken in the service of meritocracy, but operates all too often as a defense of power structures with deep imperial or corporate roots.

Curtis says: "One of the things that is stopping that change is the failure of any group to actually describe an alternative and better kind of future… they remain trapped in a mood of total distrust, constantly imagining what is being done to them as weak, manipulable individuals, rather than imagining what they as strong people can do to change the world." In his schema, all it would take to shape that narrative for real progressive change would be more idealism and enough collective will. His documentaries often tell a different tale, casting a cold eye on the history of state surveillance and social control. What if the truth is that capitalism's omnipresence and inevitability have made us all "weak, manipulable individuals" and we are simply unable to recognize this? How much worse to recognize it, but be unable to do anything about it? What if the only way to wake up to that control was to admit its existence, to understand how deeply capitalism's mechanistic, anti-life ideology controls us? Curtis talks of a "mood of inevitability" as if it could be countered with some sort of faith in the future, but then admits that such a future is radically unthinkable. Curtis the pessimist and Curtis the idealist often come into conflict in this way.

In his "New Year's address" of 2021, the revolutionary communist Bob Avakian proclaimed: "Let us dare to act to make a reality of what science reveals as possible: a radically different and far better world and future for humanity."[6] In placing the image of a better and different world in the hands of science, he arguably displays as little faith in humanity's capacity for will and agency as Curtis seems to. This is at the heart of the philosopher John Gray's argument that what we call "progress" is a temporal illusion we experience due to our short lifespans; a kind of evolutionary confirmation bias. This is why he calls faith in science, reason or progress a legacy of Christian slave morality — a secular heresy. On the secular heresies of self-described "transhumanists" he writes:

> It seems feasible that over the coming century human nature will be scientifically remodelled. If so, it will be done haphazardly, as an upshot of struggles in the murky realm where organised crime, and the hidden parts of government vie for control. If the human species is re-engineered it will not be the result of humanity assuming godlike control of its destiny. It will be another twist in man's fate.[7]

For Gray, "the good life is not found in dreams of progress, but in coping with tragic contingencies." This describes the political activity of many, many good and well-intentioned people working to ameliorate the worst effects of capitalism upon their fellow human beings. If you ask anyone working on the frontlines of

---

6   Bob Avakian, "A New Year, The Urgent Need For A Radically New World — For The Emancipation Of All Humanity," Revcom.us, Jan. 1 2021, https://revcom.us/en/avakian/new-years-statement-2021/bob-avakian-new-years-statement-2021-en.html (Accessed Feb. 4, 2024).

7   John Gray, *Straw Dogs: Thoughts on Humans and Other Animals* (Granta, 2003), p6.

society's poorest, most war-torn and dangerous regions whether a better world is possible, many would say it is. That faith in progress, and the possibility of change, obscures the tragic fact that complicity in capitalism is practically inescapable. It also obscures the illusory quality of working towards a better world under such a system, whether through reform or emergency intervention. For their utopian ambitions to be realized, the problems they are there to solve or mitigate would have to disappear completely — an impossibility in a society that already expects volunteers to plug the gaps.

As Gray quite rightly points out, science won't save us either — not by solving the problems posed by climate change, or by improving the human body to survive for longer. It's unlikely science will even achieve the dreams of immortality fervently pursued by tech giants and CEOs. Techno-optimism is never balanced by sociological cynicism outside of science fiction. The basic lie of all utopian promises derived from technology is the bare fact that most advances happen during wartime. It takes extinction-level events to significantly change human culture. That's the problem with putting your faith in nanotech and quantum computing. These are *fin-de-siecle* technologies and will most likely not be realized in any useful way until it is too late — and if they were, they would be monopolized by global elites, and so would not in any way solve the problems of wealth and resource distribution. Capitalism won't be "fixed" by technology — in all likelihood it will simply decline. What comes next is likely to be ugly.

We have the technology, but we also still have oligarchic hypercapitalism, so if the technological solutions that would bring about post-scarcity or a post-finance, post-capitalist economy existed (rather than being latent potentials, which is in itself arguable), they would either be suppressed, trademarked and ring-fenced, or in some way only made available to a rich minority. Anyone who has followed the initial utopian promise of blockchain technologies and their eventual co-option and eclipse by pyramid schemes such as cryptocurrency and NFTs will recognize this pattern. The societal and attitudinal changes needed to bring about post-scarcity are huge challenges that require more than simply having the extant tech lying around in order to solve them. The same is true of the techno-optimist's wish to transcend mortality through cyborg modification, or the "upload" of their personality into digital realms. This technology will not save humanity because it cannot even save the multi-billionaires funding it. Gray explains why:

> Cyberspace is an artefact of physical objects — computers and the networked facilities they need — not an ontologically separate reality. If the material basis of cyberspace were destroyed or severely disrupted, any minds that had been uploaded would be snuffed out… Every technology requires a physical infrastructure in order to operate. But this infrastructure depends on social institutions, which are frequently subject to breakdown… For these believers in technological resurrection, American society was already immortal… Cyberspace is a projection of the human world, not a way out of it.[8]

---

8   John Gray, "Dear Google, Please Solve Death," *New Statesman*, Apr. 9, 2017, https://www.newstatesman.com/culture/2017/04/dear-google-please-solve-death (Accessed Feb. 4, 2024).

None of the promises transhumanism makes are based on a less unfair sharing-out of resources. If anything, transhumanists believe that such acts of transcendence are the purest form of capitalist commerce. After all, the benefits will be delivered by market research and investment. Why would the product of such a process — a transhuman society — be any different, let alone fairer, or more utopian? Any and all post-human projects conceived under capitalism will reproduce capitalist ideals, as Antonella Dibiase writes in her definition of "neurocapitalism":

> Without awareness and without struggles to create lines of flight opposed to neoliberalism, there is no guarantee that we will see the birth of a different ethic… even posthumanism, assuming that we reach it one day, will remain marked by the economic rationality which currently dominates.[9]

The same is true of all our efforts to transcend, whether by changing our physical appearance, our political affiliations, our habits, or our minds. Nothing that we can create or embody implies a particular future, a particular outcome that we can control or even influence. We are less able than we think to control the present, and the physicality with which we inhabit it. The present is a place where we are constantly surveilled and controlled, yet we remain convinced, at all levels of society, that rituals of performance can offer us an escape into an imagined future, a better place. There is

---

9   Antonella DiBiase, "What is Neurocapitalism and Why Are We Living In It?" *Vice Magazine*, Oct. 16, 2016, https://www.vice.com/en/article/qkjxaq/what-is-neurocapitalism-and-why-are-we-living-in-it (Accessed Feb. 4, 2024).

no escape, not even to the fantasy of virtual realities, as Douglas Rushkoff writes:

> This "out of sight, out of mind" externalization of poverty and poison doesn't go away just because we've covered our eyes with VR goggles and immersed ourselves in an alternate reality. If anything, the longer we ignore the social, economic, and environmental repercussions, the more of a problem they become. This, in turn, motivates even more withdrawal, more isolationism and apocalyptic fantasy — and more desperately concocted technologies and business plans. The cycle feeds itself.[10]

There is no future to be had unless the present can be truly witnessed, but we have no desire to see. There is no "self" for us, beyond the narcissistic individual self under hypercapitalism. Every piece of culture we produce is just a cracked mirror for our prejudices, our naive beliefs, and our illusions — and yet we are captivated by the reflections in the glass, even when we know that beyond our gaze, in our peripheral vision the world is crumbling, and the suffering of others continues. The saddest truth is that under such a system, even to engage with the poverty, suffering and abuse in the world without a clear-eyed knowledge that your efforts are in vain is to allow yourself to slip into a solipsistic fantasy where the past is mere prologue, and the future unwritten.

---

10 Douglas Rushkoff, "Survival of the Richest," OneZero, Medium, Jul. 5, 2018, https://onezero.medium.com/survival-of-the-richest-9ef6cddd0cc1 (Accessed Feb. 4, 2024).

What if the first step to true freedom is to admit you have no control? What spaces does that open up for us in the imagination, towards John Gray's conception of "the good life"? In confronting how radically powerless we truly are, perhaps we can begin to see the need to dismantle the apparatus of control — if only to improve the present, and only for a short while. Empathy gets lost in the future, and is easily forgotten. It must be practiced in the present. The stakes have never been higher, but the wager is similar to the one Jimmy Carter took in 1977. As the anthropologist Jason Hickel puts it: "Either we evolve into a future beyond capitalism, or we won't have a future at all."[11]

Science may drive and deliver progress in the kind of measurable, statistically-provable ways so beloved of neoliberal thinkers, but there are consequences. Progress is asymmetrical. The cost of civilization is measured in poisoned oceans, skeleton coasts and cornfield tundras. It leaks catastrophically, spewing out bubonic ice and rolling death smog. Progress is conflict expressed as heat death. It is counted in jetset haloes with permafrost price tags. Its face is the drowning of ancient homelands in anoxic water feedback loops. It walks in the footsteps of displaced populations. Progress is the poisonous miasma of social fate. Technologies sustain the illusion of progress by hiding the parts of reality they do not reach — those that cannot pay for technology, or which must be exploited so that we can have our laptops and mobile phones.

We tell ourselves that these technologies are tools, that we need them in order to produce the future. What does it mean to be

---

11 Jason Hickel and Martin Kirk, "Are You Ready to Consider That Capitalism is the Real Problem?" *Fast Company*, Nov. 7, 2017, https://www. fastcompany.com/40439316/are-you-ready-to-consider-that-capitalism-is-the-real-problem (Accessed Feb. 4, 2024).

"consumers" if we really want to call ourselves "producers"? Progress, after all, is measured in the things we make, from medicines to industrial robots to artificial intelligences. It's also measured in the energy we expend to bring such monstrosities into the world. It's in the toxic runoff from our factories and the clouds of smog that rise from our vehicles. We leave the artifacts of our progress all around us, and quickly discard them to fester in trash heaps. How do we resolve these contradictions? In a 2021 conversation with the philosopher Leonardo Caffo, Slavoj Žižek returns to a proposition he first explored in 2010's *Living in the End Times*:

> What is required from us in this moment is, paradoxically, a kind of super-anthropocentrism: we should control nature, control our environment; we should allow for a reciprocal relationship to exist between the countryside and cities; we should use technology to stop desertification or the polluting of the seas. We are, once again, responsible for what is happening, and so we are also the solution.[12]

Some, like Žižek, see a kind of invidious double-bargain at play in the finality of the scientific intervention required to perhaps undo centuries of fatal production and consumption, and restore some kind of balance to the ecosystem of the planet. Others like John Gray consider "climate-hacking" interventions like cloud-seeding, carbon capture, or other such science-fiction, moonshot projects as inherently flawed, or at least as prone to error and disastrous

---

12 Quoted in Leonardo Caffo, "A Conversation with Slavoj Žižek," *Public Seminar*, Oct. 20, 2021, https://publicseminar.org/essays/a-conversation-with-slavoj-zizek (Accessed Feb. 4, 2024).

vulnerabilities as the project of transhumanism. Maybe these two positions give us the contours of the dilemma. The solutions we seek to apply to climate collapse will have their own side effects, perhaps yet more disastrous than the wreckage progress has wrought so far. The idea that we could unite on a global scale, as Žižek says, and apply a single, technologically perfect solution or series of solutions to the problem still seems impossibly utopian. The idea that science will save us rests on the fallacy that we are producers, not consumers. In truth, both activities generate their own ruin. It's an error to think the fruits of the resources we extract are borne out in the glorious light of progress; that what we make exceeds what we burn through, that it eclipses what we excrete. To that idealistic proposition, there can be only one response — look around.

Perhaps, as Natalie Wolchover writes, we are just "super-consumers who burn through enormous amounts of chemical energy, degrading it and increasing the entropy of the universe as we power the reactions in our cells."[13] It's an image that should appeal to anyone steeped in the apocalyptic, city-smashing fantasies of superhero comics. Humanity as the herald of entropy, a plague of Galactus-like beings; eaters at the edge of conceivable reality, flattening and filling the entire universe with our cosmic excrement.

---

13 Emily Wolchover, "Controversial New Theory Suggests Life Wasn't a Fluke of Biology," *Wired*, Jul. 30, 2017, https://www.wired.com/story/controversial-new-theory-suggests-life-wasnt-a-fluke-of-biologyit-was-physics (Accessed Feb. 4, 2024).

three

CASCADING CATASTROPHIC COLONY COLLAPSE

> In truth, we have only one foot in the natural environ-
> ment of this world. Other worlds are always calling us
> away from nature. We live in a habitat of unrealities
> — not of earth, air, water and wildlife — and cradling
> illusion trounces grim logic every time.[1]
>
> —Thomas Ligotti
> *The Conspiracy Against The Human Race*

A 2014 NASA study on climate change, quoted in *The Atlan-tic*, concludes with the bold assertion that "collapse can be avoided, and population can reach a steady state at the maximum carrying capacity, if the rate of depletion of nature is reduced to a sustainable level, and if resources are distributed equitably."[2] This is perhaps as true as saying that if they could just generate enough thrust, pigs could fly. While both statements are possible, neither is provable or probable. Rather, as anthropologist Jason Hickel writes, it is time to confront some uncomfortable truths: "It was unthinkable to say this even 10 years ago, but today, as we become increasingly aware of these crises, it seems all too clear: our

---

1   Thomas Ligotti, *The Conspiracy Against The Human Race* (Hippocampus Press, 2010), p78.

2   Alex Brown, "Here's how NASA thinks society will collapse," *The Atlantic*, Mar. 18, 2014, https://www.theatlantic.com/politics/archive/2014/03/her-es-how-nasa-thinks-society-will-collapse/441375 (Accessed Feb. 10, 2024).

economic system is incompatible with life on this planet."[3] The vector for the end of human civilization is not just political, cultural or technological — it is also biological in the strictest sense. All populations, whether human or animal, eventually collapse. This is as much of a fact as the eventual heat death of the sun. Furthermore, collapse does not always imply rebirth or regrowth. Sometimes, things that are destined to collapse are more like a series of dominoes. One push, and everything will cascade. All living things on the planet are subject to this law. There is little reason to presume human beings are the exception.

A paper published in 2022 by Niggli, Huggel, Muccione, Neukom and Salzmann studies the "interconnectedness" of environmental, economic, infrastructural, cultural, and medical systems. They conclude that cascade effects are poorly understood, inevitable, and already underway: "Cascading impacts can propagate through numerous sectors with far-reaching consequences, potentially being able to destabilize entire socio-economic systems,"[4] the authors write. Their analysis of the ways in which human systems are linked, affecting each other in statistically predictable ways that are as yet under-appreciated or researched, focuses on the impact of extreme weather events, unstable energy markets, infrastructure collapse, and social unrest. These all produce measurable effects, which are interrelated:

---

3   Jason Hickel, "To Deal With Climate Change We Need a New Financial System," *The Guardian*, Nov. 5, 2016, https://www.theguardian.com/global-development-professionals-network/2016/nov/05/how-a-new-money-system-could-help-stop-climate-change (Accessed Feb. 10, 2024).

4   Laura Niggli et al., "Towards Improved Understanding of Cascading and Interconnected Risks from Concurrent Weather Extremes," *PLoS*, Aug. 10, 2022, https://journals.plos.org/climate/article?id=10.1371/journal.pclm.0000057 (Accessed Feb. 10, 2024).

> The sectors most affected by direct impacts of heat and drought extremes are the health sector and the agriculture and food production sector. In addition, the energy sector, the transport and mobility sector as well as the economy and financial system are also strongly affected if indirect effects that emerge from cascading impacts are also taken into account. Sectors that were given less attention in the analyzed literature, but have themselves strong potential to affect other sectors are water resources, ecosystems as well as critical infrastructure and buildings… Eventually, all impacts propagating through the system can be expected in one way or another to end up compromising the economy, the state and public services and thus society and culture.

Extreme weather events and the unpreparedness of our governments and societies to deal with their consequences are only part of the picture, of course, and the study does not consider other factors that could contribute to a cascade. John Gray has written extensively about animal birth rates, population pressure, and the way in which the quite natural, asymmetrical decline and fall of species is unlikely to be a fate humanity escapes by dint of technological or social "progress." These cascade effects precede the collapse of colonies in ways that are sometimes poorly understood in animal populations, but are almost universally present.

Humans will become extinct, as all animals must, and there is no reason to presume that this could not happen in the near term. The potential for cascading climate chaos to contribute to or cause a collapse (or series of interconnected collapses) of our infrastructure and societies at large is simply an increased risk factor for a fate that is inevitable over the long term. This is also true of Western, liberal democracy. There is simply no reason to presume that it will continue to survive, let alone to evolve in such a way as to widen and expand democratic franchises and personal freedoms, or ensure the survival of the human beings under its purview and care — especially in the face of climate collapse. As John Gray writes:

> Ways of life come to an end for a number of reasons. They can be wiped out by repression and genocide, or rendered unviable by technology or economic change. The regimes that protect them may lose power in wars and revolutions. In some cases, though, they die from exhaustion or boredom. The moderately liberal way of life… may be one of these cases.[5]

The NASA study concludes with an almost religious assertion of the collective will and power of a globally united humanity, but the argument that our democratic institutions will continue to operate as functional societal norms is shakier than it used to be, even in mainstream liberal discourse (as the later study by Niggli et al. confirms with chilling clarity). If society collapses, a turn towards authoritarian strongmen (or worse) seems a logical progression. The right has always threatened the disappearance or destruction of rights and property — this is its leverage at the ballot box. The more real this threat becomes, the more votes they

---

5   John Gray, "The Myth of Natural Morality," *New Statesman*, Nov. 25, 2020, https://www.newstatesman.com/ideas/2020/11/whats-wrong-with-rights-nigel-biggar-review (Accessed Feb. 10, 2024).

will attract, for as long as voting is permitted. Recent history has provided many challenges, not least of which is the right's willingness to capitulate to, and even celebrate naked authoritarianism. It is naive to assume that this will not continue as the societal chaos caused by climate collapse intensifies.

"Incoherent societies cannot formulate coherent strategies,"[6] as Gray argues. The shared center ground on which progress is supposed to rest is fragile now, and perhaps always has been. In the UK, the moderate social democratic gains seen after the Second World War have been eroded and undermined, first by decades of boom-and-bust neoliberal economics, then a decade or more of austerity. Trust in politicians is low, and partisan lines are firmly drawn. As critic and journalist Henry A. Giroux puts it:

> As the social sphere is emptied of democratic institutions and ideals, apocalyptic visions of fear and fatalism reinforce the increasingly normalised assumption that there are no alternatives to existing political logics and the tyranny of a neoliberal global economy.[7]

Polarised swings between authoritarian populism and cautious neoliberalism seem to be all we can hope for from democratic nations in the near term. If so, consensus and progress are failed projects, and the liberal world is no longer an exemplar of

---

6   John Gray, "What Sun Tzu Knew," *New Statesman*, Jan. 29, 2020, https://www.newstatesman.com/long-reads/2020/01/sun-tzu-the-art-war-politics (Accessed Feb. 10, 2024).

7   Henry A. Giroux, "Depoliticization Is a Deadly Weapon of Neoliberal Fascism," *Truthout*, Feb. 15, 2019, https://truthout.org/articles/depoliticization-is-a-deadly-weapon-of-neoliberal-fascism (Accessed Feb. 10, 2024).

human achievement, let alone its savior. In such conditions, the adaptation, cooperation, and agility required on a global scale to respond effectively to climate collapse seem all but impossible, or at the very least, unlikely to spring from that source. As we have seen since the turn of the twenty-first century, each successive government tends to wipe the board of the achievements of its predecessor anyway — but these bold sweeps, particularly when they involve the erosion of democratic norms, do nothing to challenge the dominance of neoliberal and hypercapitalist economic logic. More often, they reaffirm and strengthen it, or hand more power over to corporate influence. There's no progress because there's no policy outside capitalist realism, or at least not for long enough to make a difference — even if it can escape the bounds of what the so-called "free market" deems possible. What looks like progress is in fact stasis.

When we confront this contradictory gap between our belief in progress and the lack of evidence for it, we tend to contradict ourselves, and multiply the error. For example, the Swedish author Andreas Malm admits that we're facing "a situation of deepening scarcity of a lot of critical bio-physical resources,"[8] a belief that has informed his academic writing about climate change. His research has led him towards the conclusion that only some form of communism might confront and ameliorate that scarcity, but as is so often the case, what he actually proposes is to fine-tune the controls of hypercapitalism: "We must say that some forms of consumption are non-essential and outright destructive... and

---

8   George Eaton, "Andreas Malm: The Likely Future is Escalating Catastrophe," *New Statesman*, Oct. 14, 2020, https://www.newstatesman.com/encounter/2020/10/andreas-malm-likely-future-escalating-catastrophe (Accessed Feb. 10, 2024).

these forms will have to be regulated." By the time we have regulated and campaigned our way to Malm's functional communist society, everyone will be dead.

It's almost as if we cannot see society at the collective level anymore. The mass political movements, and before them the major religions, allowed for a type of collective thinking that has rapidly disappeared in the past half-century — first into a blindly acquisitive individualism, and now a narcissistic inner focus that privileges the personal above the political, the communal, global or environmental. We believe in our inner lives more than we believe in the lives of others, or in the external world. Critic Siddartha Deb describes the way this operates in narrative fiction:

> Fiction suffers from its own kind of anthropocenization, one that owes as much to post-war prosperity in the West and to globalisation, which succeeded in universalizing the obsession with individuals, character, and interiority that dominates writing programs and its reviewing culture. Even nature, resource extraction, and climate change, viewed through the filter of character, become a kind of exoticizing backdrop.[9]

As narcissistic heroes of the era of climate collapse, we are dedicated to a kind of cosplay of "averting the end times" while we glorify ourselves on social media for our actions. We are perhaps no less guilty of imposing an unhelpful and dominant cultural narrative on those who experience the worst effects of climate change than imperial colonizers were when they subjected

---

9   Siddartha Deb, "Stranger Than Fiction," *The Baffler*, Jun. 5, 2017, https://thebaffler.com/contraband/stranger-than-fiction (Accessed Feb.10, 2024).

indigenous populations to cultural (and literal) genocide. As the indigenous activist Nemonte Nenquimo writes:

> My elders are my teachers. The forest is my teacher… You forced your civilization upon us and now look where we are: global pandemic, climate crisis, species extinction and, driving it all, widespread spiritual poverty. In all these years of taking, taking, taking from our lands, you have not had the courage, or the curiosity, or the respect to get to know us.[10]

The catastrophism that drives our obsession with aestheticized apocalypses is the same delusion that powers our belief that the meager concessions we make towards recycling and fair trade will bring about equality and climate justice (let alone utopia). What progress we have made — in our technology, our culture — has already damned us. How can we believe more of it will save us? The extreme weather events, fires, infectious disease outbreaks, heatwaves, sea level rises and flooding we have witnessed in recent years will continue to intensify as we approach the threshold of a two-degree rise in the global temperature.[11] While the declining nations of the democratic West may currently see

---

10 Nemonte Nenquimo, "This is My Message to the Western World - Your Civilisation is Killing Life on Earth," *The Guardian*, Oct. 12, 2020, https://www.theguardian.com/commentisfree/2020/oct/12/western-worldyour-civilisation-killing-life-on-earth-indigenous-amazon-planet (Accessed Feb.10, 2024).

11 See another NASA study: Taejin Park et al., "What Does Global Land Climate Look Like at 2°C Warming?" Dec. 20, 2022 *Advanced Earth and Space Sciences*, https://agupubs.onlinelibrary.wiley.com/doi/10.1029/2022EF003330 (Accessed Feb. 10, 2024).

these events as happening in distant places where those they have othered are unfortunate enough to live, their proximity can only increase, and has demonstrably increased with time. As the writer Travis Reider puts it: "The global poor will be hurt first and worst… Hundreds of millions, if not billions of people could become climate refugees, as their homelands become uninhabitable."[12] This process is already underway, and more advanced than most people allow themselves to believe.

If utopia and catastrophism often go hand in hand, the theories of "deep adaptation" (proposed by Jem Bendell) and "deep ecology" (originated by Arnae Næss) can be misread as justifying ecofascism. The specter of a world beset by tidal migrations of refugees against a backdrop of collapsing states and chaotic, existential weather threats lends itself to the persona and obsessions of the backwoods crank or the doomsday prepper. Fuelled by the post-apocalypse aesthetics of zombie fiction like *The Walking Dead*, the right-wing conspiracist can easily see peaceful and Stoic philosophies like those of Bendell and Naess as some sort of prescient science fiction how-to guide, adding layers of racial violence and "justified" home defense to the exhortations to grow one's own crops, and become comfortable with the idea of the end of society. These are Ted Kaczynski's children.

Without narratives to understand the reality of the asymmetrical collapse that has already begun in our environment and in our societies, we risk playing the dupe for both extremes of this argument. We can deny the reality of the huge stress the human

---

12 Travis Reider, "Why We Should Have Fewer Children to Save the Planet," *The Guardian*, Sep. 12, 2016, https://www.theguardian.com/commentisfree/2016/sep/12/why-we-should-have-fewer-children-save-the-planet-climate-change (Accessed Feb. 10, 2024).

population places on the natural world. We can embrace that reality and disappear into some fantasy where our actions can mitigate or avoid the absolute certainty of the promised collapse. It's that, or a cabin in the woods, a bunker in the backyard … a fire at a cave mouth, sticks pointed outwards to stave off the sharp-toothed terrors the night holds. None of these positions lead to a resolution, let alone action. They are fantasies — denial, or barbarism.

Any discussion of climate change is inherently a discussion of resource distribution, and yet mainstream discourse, research and policy all too often attempt to separate the issues. While the planet burns, its resources dwindle often *because* of inequalities in resource distribution. As the study by Niggli et al. demonstrates, food and power supply chains are all too vulnerable to war or extreme weather. War in Ukraine, droughts in Norway and France, wildfires in Greece, Canada and the United States — at the time of writing, all of these can and have led to a cost of living crisis, soaring energy bills, and the poverty and immiseration of millions. These crises are underwritten by a neoliberal class who believe it is ethical to balance human lives against the needs of shareholders. These are exactly the kinds of supply chain issues the study analyzed, and they underline our vulnerability and powerlessness as capitalist subjects. The number of citizens capitalism would throw upon the gears to oil the machine with blood is infinite — because there is no alternative for the elite. They do not care if we starve and die. As the writer and journalist Joshua Ellis put it in a prescient 2016 Facebook post:

> All of human endeavour can be understood as a race between how fast we consume and how fast we can replace or provide. And none of our resources are

really infinite — sunlight is the closest, but even that
has a shelf life, though nobody will almost certainly
be around to see it… This is what the real endgame
of consumer capitalism looks like, because it cannot
control itself: a wasteland and starving masses. Everything else is just the floor show. And the floor show,
no matter how diverting and charming, must always
end, and so must every *belle epoque*.[13]

There has never been a greater need for pragmatic realism
about the facts of climate collapse, and how those are likely to
affect our societies. Studies like the one quoted here by Niggli et
al. are a start, but even they cannot prepare us for the prospect of
the complete erasure and disappearance of our ways of life, and
the end of the prosperous, democratic "*belle epoque*," as Ellis puts
it. Nothing is safe — not the weak and vulnerable people our neoliberal societies pretend to protect, nor the democratic traditions
and ideologies that supposedly still underwrite this protection.
We have already failed to protect ourselves, let alone others, from
this onslaught. Perhaps the fall of our culture is assured one way
or another. The writing's on the wall, as the "planetary futurist"
Alex Steffen puts it:

If we don't get smart enough, fast enough, people are
going to get left behind, especially in places which are
already perceived to have limited value, like run-down
cities, bankrupt suburbs and poor rural areas. If the
past decade is any indication, neither government nor

---

13 Quoted from a post on a personal Facebook account by permission of the
author, Joshua Ellis (https://www.patreon.com/jzellis).

industry is going to be riding in to help restore critical
systems in a timely manner...[14]

Smart enough, fast enough — these too are descriptions that
depend on faith, in a belief that we can learn and act. Is there
not enough evidence yet to show that we have learned, but we
will not act? Futurists like Steffen write about these scenarios as
if they were imagined, *Mad Max* futures, when they are already
here. They are present in the disrepair and impoverishment of
urban communities; the gun-ravaged inner cities of Detroit and
Chicago, or the burning Paris *banlieues*. They can be observed
in dead Midwestern rust belt towns with lead in their water, or
run-down former mining villages in the north of England gutted
by Thatcherite economic logic. They are present in the so-called
third or developing world, where heat, disease and drought are
already major causes of suffering and death. These populations
are already "left behind" and climate change is already impacting
them first, and hardest.

If climate collapse continues and global temperatures
increase, even the 1.5°C increase set down as a maximum target under the terms of the Paris Accords would see significant
sections of Europe's population, before the century ends, living
under conditions currently experienced in the deep desert.[15]
Mounting evidence suggests that even these predictions are

---

14 Alex Steffen, "The Outquisition," Medium, Jun. 16, 2016, https://
   medium.com/@AlexSteffen/the-outquisition-3e15cb889032 (Accessed
   Feb. 10, 2024).

15 See a study by the European Court of Auditors: "Combating Desertification in the EU," Publications Office of the European Union,
   2018, https://op.europa.eu/webpub/eca/special-reports/desertifica-
   tion-33-2018/en/ (Accessed Feb. 10, 2024).

conservative, and may not take into account the multiplying effects of feedback loops within weather systems, air purity, crop cycles and sea conditions (factors not considered in the study by Niggli et al., which focused on the interaction between the *effects* of such extreme weather events, rather than the events themselves). We simply do not know how things will change, or how fast. What we do know may well be tainted by the secular heresy of our belief in progress. The small niche of geological time in which the human race has existed was dependent on a certain range of climate conditions. We have now passed out of that range, and into new territories. If we expect our cultures and societies to survive such a shift, we may presume too much. Other species become extinct when their environment is destroyed, when population pressure causes disease or infertility to increase, or when they are replaced by a better-adapted organism. For human beings standing on the lip of this new century, all of these preconditions are now realities, or soon could be.

four

MEME WAR

> Human spirit is a kind of virus that parasitizes on the human animal, exploits it for its own self-reproduction, and sometimes threatens to destroy it.[1]
> —Slavoj Žižek
> *Pandemic! Covid 19 shakes the world*

In John Barnes' violent, uncompromising and prescient 1995 cyberpunk novel *Kaleidoscope Century* a young man is recruited as a sleeper agent by a crumbling Soviet network of spies and saboteurs in the US known as "the Organisation." The novel follows a parallel timeline. When the USSR begins to collapse, a new and more militaristic form of state communism topples the slowly Western-capitulating administration. Boris Yeltsin is executed live on television. As the new post-Soviet power emerges, it is clear that any ties to ideological or state communism are gone. The American protagonist begins to work for the Organisation as a destabilizing "black ops" agent, sabotaging and strategically murdering political, military and civilian targets in America and beyond.

In what feels like a callback to the dummy President of Philip K. Dick's *Valis*,[2] it is heavily implied that this new, anti-democratic Russian power is behind the election of a puppet leader in the US, whose extended term, ably assisted by the covert action of sleeper

---

1   Slavoj Žižek, *Pandemic! Covid 19 shakes the world* (Polity, 2020), p79.
2   Philip K. Dick, *Valis* (Bantam Books, 1981).

agents like our hero, signals the end of the US as a democracy. The parallels to the ascendancy and chaotic reign of Donald Trump and his shadow ties to the post-Soviet, gangster-state proto-fascism of Vladimir Putin's Russia are self-evidently prophetic. But what is fascinating about the novel nearly thirty years on from its publication is not how uncannily it mirrors our own age of emergent political and social collapse, but where Barnes predicts the future of warfare, espionage, artificial intelligence and ecological devastation might lead. No other science fiction writer has captured this confluence of threats as vividly.

The unnamed (or rather, multi-named) protagonist of *Kaleidoscope Century* is a sleeper agent in Barnes' alt-history present day, but we learn of this in atemporal, nonlinear fragments. The novel opens in a "Marshack" on the red planet 100 years in the future, as the protagonist tries to piece together memories from the digital fragments on his "werp" (a device that is halfway between a laptop and a mobile phone). Barnes slowly unfolds the timeline of his amnesiac narrator's life, jumping in and out of different identities, eras and phases of human history and society, aided by life-extending drugs provided by the Organisation.

There are moments of utter brutality in the book — Barnes' characters are morally bereft to the point of barbarity, and beyond. In one section, the narrator and his sometime friend, sometime enemy Sadi are employed to entrap US politicians by throwing a drug-fuelled orgy at a diplomatic residence in Prague. As rumors of an attack on the city spread, the pair further destabilize the situation by goading the orgy into a frenzy of violence, rape, and murder. The scene is chilling, but feels utterly real — a snapshot of how violence, especially sexual violence, is used in conflict and espionage.

Such brutality serves a point in the book — in a collapsing world, the narrator is not just an amoral double agent, he is also perfectly prepared to come to terms with the worst imaginable depths of human depravity in order to get paid and survive. Yet as the narrator switches back into the present, he feels appalled. Piecing together his memories from the "werp," he doubts his account of events. They horrify him; he weeps, he regrets. But he can no more deny that he perpetrated these atrocities than he can be absolutely sure they took place. His memories are a kaleidoscope.

While the narrator begins as a kind of secret agent, the life-extension drugs he takes enable him to take up a new identity every few decades. At each point of re-emergence, he experiences amnesia, and must piece together the fragments of his past lives, the new social and cultural (or often, military) situation in which he has re-awoken. This journey will take him from service as a spy to become a private military contractor, a construction worker, a Mars prospector, and finally a fugitive. The nature, allegiance and ideology of the Organisation changes; sometimes it disappears. Eventually though, the Organisation always finds him, and he is recruited again. The journey begins in the world of shadowy, outsourced counterintelligence work. Barnes' unfolds a narrative that speaks to what Richard Hosfstadter, in 1964, identified as the "paranoid style" in American politics:

> The paranoid spokesman sees the fate of conspiracy in
> apocalyptic terms - he traffics in the birth and death of
> whole worlds, whole political orders, whole systems
> of human values. He is always manning the barricades
> of civilization. He constantly lives at a turning point.
> Like religious millennialists he expresses the anxiety

of those who are living through the last days and he is sometimes disposed to set a date for the apocalypse.[3]

Barnes, like all great American science fiction authors, is a paranoid spokesman for the counterculture. He portrays a world in which the two great "paranoid" powers — the USA and the former USSR — are slowly and covertly merged behind the scenes into a single corporate, globe-spanning entity. This takes place via espionage, and a mixture of outright and clandestine conflict. His narrator is an amoral agent in the middle of this war between "good" and "evil." He comes to realize that neither side is in it for anything except power. The "paranoid style" is at once the source of Barnes' anxieties, expressed in the plot, and the backdrop to his vision of apocalypse.

From here, the planet descends into what Barnes calls "The War of the Memes." The barricades of civilization are not manned in the name of humanity, but in the name of domination. The paranoid style — the engine of conflict that drove the Cold War — becomes merely a competition between powerful and identically authoritarian blocs, which eventually become even larger, merged monopolies. Authoritarianism becomes the dominant form not through the ballot box, but through the secret machinations of an unaccountable elite. There are echoes here of the capture of the Republican Party by the shadow-narrative of Q-Anon, and on a lesser scale, the shady backroom dealings with Russian oligarchs undertaken by the Tory Party. While ostensibly we still vote and participate in a democracy, in practice, corporate and

---

3   Richard Hofstadter, "The Paranoid Style in American Politics," *Harpers*, 1964, https://harpers.org/archive/1964/11/the-paranoid-style-in-american-politics (Accessed Feb. 10, 2024).

elite interests take precedence. This truth is expressed in the real world via the fantasy of conspiracy theories. A network of shadow-power *is* protected at the highest levels. This is unfortunate, because it maps conveniently onto events such as the death of Jeffrey Epstein. Whether his fate was an accident or self-inflicted, it fits the pattern identified by paranoid narratives like Q-Anon, and as such, is taken as evidence. As Sarah Churchwell writes:

> Paranoid narratives are inherently narcissistic as well as authoritarian. Paranoia rejects the proportionality of pluralism, in which the world's indifference to you is a sign of its multiplicity, and interprets that indifference as malice. The world is not unmoved by your existence, but upholds your central importance: even your refrigerator is spying on you. A paranoid system confirms that your powerlessness is only because the game is rigged against you – and that the world cares enough to bother disempowering you.[4]

All paranoid narratives contain a grain of truth. While the heroes of the ultimate "paranoid" SF writer, Philip K. Dick, are often powerless as they discover the horrific reality or the "secret chiefs" of his fictional worlds, the hero of *Kaleidoscope Century* is an agent of that power; he is the perpetrator of those horrors. He is the character who would have slipped a makeshift noose around Epstein's neck to protect the secrets of his paymasters. Barnes portrays him

---

4   Sarah Churchwell, "Can American Democracy Survive Donald Trump?" *The Guardian*, Nov. 21, 2020, https://www.theguardian.com/books/2020/nov/21/can-american-democracy-survive-donald-trump (Accessed Feb.10, 2024).

as completely amoral, opportunistic, and utterly prepared to use terror and brutality to achieve the mission objective, so he can get paid.

As Barnes unfolds a future that proceeds from such a para-noid world, the Organisation begins to recede. Climate collapse leads to global conflict, but as regional and national borders become more irrelevant, the warring divisions split along cultural lines. For these "mass contagions" of ideological and spiritual conformity, Barnes uses the term coined by Richard Dawkins — memes. There are the Ecucatholics, the Cybertao, the liber-tarian, anti-meme Freecybers, and the increasingly dominant One True; a nascent version of what will come to be known as "Resuna," the meme that will eventually dominate and absorb all other memes. Resuna is portrayed by Barnes as a consciousness, not unlike Skynet from 1984's *The Terminator*. It is a malignant artificial intelligence dedicated only to its own proliferation, and the control of the human population. Unlike Skynet, which is a distributed "neural net" of nodes that exists in connected com-puters, Resuna exists in the collective consciousness of humanity. It cannot be switched off.

Barnes' "memes" are ideological or spiritual movements that mutate into a communal consciousness — a mass of programmed humanity in thrall to larger cultural "entities"; a techno-cult. As ideologies and nations disappear, religion-like ideas rise again, but in a toxic, techno-augmented form. These "memes" behave as nothing less than monopolistic corporate entities. The price of "joining" one is your individuality — an unpleasant process of infection that overwrites your personality. The War of the Memes is at once a physical conflict between small, technolog-ically advanced paramilitary units, conducted in and amongst

civilian populations, and a conflict of "ideas" waged by large reli-
gious-corporate military "brands." These ideas, however, are not
ideologies (or at least, not anymore). The warring memes have no
goal beyond their own reproduction. Human beings are merely
a vector for their evolution and continuing existence. Artificial
intelligence, weapons technology, and the "memes" that drive the
conflict become one and the same thing:

> The war had been raging ever since some bright guy
> had figured out how to write a program that could ana-
> lyze any operating system it talked to, figure out how to
> penetrate it, and get in and take over AIs. Whoever it
> was, he'd probably never realized that to a program like
> that, a mind's just one more operating system running
> on a slow-running massively parallel processor.[5]

Even the Freecybers, the "anti-meme" memes designed to keep
individuals free, become instruments of conformity and control,
as Sadi explains after he and the narrator kill two renegade Freecy-
ber agents:

> Everything out there in the noosphere mutates pretty
> fast. Whatever they started out to do, I think the
> Freecybers are probably just like any other memes
> now, replicating because they can, spreading out any
> old way, taking over and running things, no doubt
> believing themselves to have the best of intentions…
> That's the reason we had to kill them. Not just that
> One True would have taken them over, but that they'd

---

have found out they were wrong, and I wanted them to believe right to the end.[6]

Sadi and the narrator, who kill on behalf of the memes, are also afraid of them. Broadcasts of memetic information that scramble human personalities and enforce the individual's sublimation into the memetic "whole" are demonstrated by Barnes as violent psychic attacks; a psychotic break delivered through broadcast devices (early "werps"). While the novel predates the rise of social media, smartphones, and "viral" content by almost a decade, the scene where Sadi and the narrator are infected by a OneTrue meme, and immediately attempt to murder each other, is strangely reminiscent of friends watching a TikTok dance video and copying the moves. What else is a dance routine, but an idea in search of a host?[7]

Barnes' vision of memes as weaponized cultural units that evolve into cold, ruthless super-intelligences is the dark side of psychologist Susan Blackmore's mechanistic vision of human culture and behavior, as outlined in her 1999 book *The Meme Machine*,[8] shortly after the publication of Barnes' novel. In Barnes'

---

6   Barnes, *Kaleidoscope Century*, p50.
7   It has been suggested that TikTok is already a vector for "social contagion" that can be viewed as memetic in nature. A 2021 article in *Wired* outlines concerns that doctors and researchers raised around the increase of teenage girls presenting with Tourette's syndrome (and the criticism of these concerns): https://www.wired.co.uk/article/tiktok-tourettes (Accessed Feb. 11 2024).
8   Blackmore's book is a refinement and extension of Richard Dawkins' original work on memes. Blackmore later established what she calls a "third replicator" at work in human evolution — technological memes, or "temes" (first introduced in a TED lecture of 2008, *Memes and Temes*). This concept overlaps nicely with the co-evolution of memes and tech-

stark conclusion, Resuna eventually absorbs all the competing memes, and the people in their thrall. The narrator is one of a small handful of un-memed humans who leave Earth in order to remain individuals, and not become part of Resuna. It's a devastating metaphor for religion and ideological control, but perhaps also carries an echo of the "red scare" propaganda Barnes himself grew up with. In his vision of the future, communal humanity is the face of totalitarian horror. Ideas and ideology become meaningless in the furnace of forced conformity and the extermination of individuality and free will.

During the War of the Memes, Barnes also draws on several "black swan" scenarios, perhaps inspired by the work of K. Eric Drexler, the author of the 1986 book *Engines of Creation.*[9] Various world powers employ bioweapons and nanotechnological warfare in the lead-up to the war, delivering crop blights, such as "Tailored Rice Blast." Barnes' master-stroke, in terms of the novel's world-building, is that the emergent memes spring from the same technological font as the devastating ecological consequences of biowar. Both are derived from the semi-autonomous weapons he calls SMOTs (Simulation Modelling Optimising Targeters), which begin as smart weapon targeting systems, then become bioweapons:

---

nology in *Kaleidoscope Century*, although Blackmore believes that such "tremes" will bring about a utopian third industrial revolution, rather than the end of the world. See Susan Blackmore, *The Meme Machine* (Oxford University Press, 1999).

9   Drexler's book (*Engines of Creation: The Coming Era of Nanotechnology*, Doubleday, 1986) lays out both the transformative potential of nanotechnology, and the very real dangers it poses.

The SMOTs running on thousands of microsupers in tiny little labs, a few freshly-trained microbiologists in each one, wrote script after script for ecological disaster. Here a new fungus to attack a particular set of roots; there a bacteria that locked up soil phosphorus in an unusable form for a few weeks out of each growing season. Here the super-grasshopper, toxic to birds and especially attractive to them; there beetles that fed only on the leaf buds of trees in the spring. Everywhere, as vegetation lost its grip, mud and slime replaced soil, and the living parts of the continents bled down into the ocean.[10]

Ultimately, the bioweapons hack human nervous systems, and memes merge with artificial intelligence. The idea that a confluence of AI, biotechnology, and smart weapons could bring about the end of humanity feels terrifyingly plausible. The bioweapons devastate the ecosystem and reproduce just like the memes, turning cornfields into tundra and killing billions in a perverse echo of Stalin's "five year plans" and Mao's "great leap forward." In the 1990s, when Barnes was writing, such a scenario was straight out of speculative science. Now, the prospect of mass crop failures caused or exacerbated by human intervention in the food cycle with pesticides, or the use of genetically modified material and other technological "solutions" (not to mention the effects of runaway climate change) are very real considerations. The response of the governments in the novel includes solutions now recognizable in the "climate hacking" approaches often touted as remedies to climate collapse. As Barnes quite rightly

---

10 Barnes, *Kaleidoscope Century*, p114.

predicts, these may also have unintended and devastating consequences, just like the plans of Mao and Stalin.

The replacement of humanity's individuality with the total mind-control and unity of the triumphant meme, Resuna, has echoes in Joe Haldeman's classic space opera *Forever War*[11] cycle, begun in 1974. In Haldeman's Vietnam War-inspired novels, the protagonist eventually returns to Earth to find it ruled by a collective consciousness. Like Barnes' protagonist, Haldeman's hero is a man out of time. In both works, the terror expressed at this form of human unity relates to a loss of self, of individuality. Haldeman's fears betray an existential dread about common humanity-without-agency through the eyes of a rugged, individualistic hero. Barnes' concerns are expressed through a much more conflicted narrator — a man who has committed atrocities, but can only remember fragments of them.

The loss of the individual "self" to some sort of "replacement" species has long been a theme of science fiction, and there are countless robot or artificial intelligence versions of the racist "Great Replacement" theory to draw upon if we want to catastrophize about the rise of the machines. What Barnes makes clear is that the evolution of artificial intelligence will happen in concert with social changes in human culture in perhaps unpredictable ways, just as John Gray argues in *Straw Dogs*. As mentioned in an earlier chapter, John Gray writes that progress will proceed "haphazardly, as an upshot of struggles in the murky realm where organized crime, and the hidden parts of government vie for control."[12] Some hybridity, some cyborg merger of human and

---

11 Joe Haldeman, *The Forever War* (St Martin's Press, 1974).

12 John Gray, *Straw Dogs: Thoughts on Humans and Other Animals* (Granta, 2003), p6.

artificial intelligence may be inevitable — Barnes makes the argument that this will be more likely to take the form of co-evolution through subjugation, rather than the transhumanist ideal of "uploading the self" into some great digital hereafter.

The tech in Barnes' novel is appealingly battered and dysfunctional. The contents of the "werp" are like a description of the "selves" we archive now on social media, in the cloud, and on our phones. Barnes plays with the idea that these images, videos and fragments have meaning, although one obscured by time, leaving nothing but the images themselves. The motif of a fractured, broken man sifting through digital echoes he half remembers, while exiled from the world, is a perfect evocation of the way we interact with social media. Even our most animated moments — the adrenaline rush of an argument, the laugh out loud at clever memes — are experienced passively, and then quickly gone. Faced with an old image, an old video, we might scratch our heads and wonder, obscurely, if we have seen it before — if the self it portrays is truly "us."

The novel's conclusion strays into even more experimental science fiction territory, as the protagonist reunites with his longtime best friend and occasional enemy, Sadi. Now in a woman's body, Sadi explains that at around the time the narrator's story began, the Organisation created a "closed timelike curve" by detonating a large nuclear explosion on the dark side of the moon. A hole in spacetime was opened, connecting the future of 2109 with the past of 1991. Barnes' alternate history is a loop. Sadi has traveled through the time-looped pocket universe many, many times, and in that process, has gained complete control of the Organisation, up to and including the protagonist's recruitment. History has become their playground — they can live infinite lives or versions of lives, be any gender or identity they choose, kill with impunity, experience fabulous wealth or the deepest depravity they can imagine. The twenty-first century has become Sadi's "kaleidoscope" — a smorgasbord of turbulent history, a banquet of experience set against the decline and collapse of the human race. The narrator and Sadi make love, and Sadi offers him a ship to travel back through the entrance to the closed timelike curve. Like Sadi, he can experience the kaleidoscope century as many times as he wants, in as many configurations as he can imagine, before he returns to his lover's arms. Like the protagonist of *Groundhog Day* he can repeat history until he gets it "right" — but may first indulge his instincts for gluttony, hedonism and cruelty, or charity and kindness: "I can party for a hundred years. I can kill someone every month just for fun. And if it ever starts to look too hot for me, I can always get on this ship again."[13]

This conclusion struck me as powerfully strange upon my first reading of the novel. With time, the meaning has come into focus. Endless variations of gender, race, age, class, experience, suffering, delight — these are the promises of late capitalism; that we can choose our own adventure, be whatever we want to be. In practice, the consequences of this freedom liberate us from considering the individual worth of other beings with less control, other unchosen lives — including the global organism of our planet. They make us, like Sadi, into tyrants. Barnes asks if we, too, could live through collapse in a selfish and narcissistic trance, blind to our own cruelty; or at least indifferent to the suffering we cause, unable to face or imagine a future that is not a vision of totalitarian horror.

---

13 Barnes, *Kaleidoscope Century*, p252.

Like the rich, endlessly re-born oligarchs of Richard Morgan's *Altered Carbon*, eventually, Barnes' protagonist and his lover will face the "Methuselah problem." Eternal life's greatest challenge is boredom, and the moral decay that it engenders. Such disregard for consequences, for human life, makes one inhuman in a different way. Rather than abrogating control to a larger entity, subsuming themselves in the whole, they consider the world their playground, and people their playthings. Lost in sensation, they will not realize that eventually, the sensations will dull. They will become so powerful, and so removed from human experience, that they will not feel a thing. The freedom to create oneself, to choose one's destiny, is also the freedom to consider the dreams, hopes and welfare of others as less important, beneath consideration. We choose individualism, but are we driven towards meme war? Neither outcome seems destined to make us happy, or to guarantee our survival.

five

GAME OF DRONES

The cameras have invaded my thoughts. I have never vandalized the hallways of my building and never would, but since the cameras came, I think about how much I would like to, but can't because they're watching, so I stop myself from thinking about vandalizing the hallways, and then I feel oppressed and controlled. The cameras created a thought in my mind and then censored that thought. Sometimes it's hard to know, in the presence of the cameras, which thoughts belong to me and which ones belong to them.[1]

—Jeremiah Moss

*N*ew Statesman editor and contributor Jerry Cliffe writes: "The logic of any panopticon is not just to monitor but to influence the behavior of those being monitored."[2] He asks whether we want "panopticons or pandemics." This implication follows the thrust of a theoretical paper authored by Nick Bostrom, the originator of the (in)famous "Simulation Argument"

---

1   Jeremiah Moss, "Open House: Welcome to New York, Now Go Home," *N Plus One*, 2020, https://www.nplusonemag.com/issue-36/essays/open-house (Accessed Feb. 11, 2024).

2   Jerry Cliffe, "The Rise of the Bio-surveillance State," *New Statesman*, Mar. 25, 2020, https://www.newstatesman.com/long-reads/2020/03/rise-bio-surveillance-state (Accessed Feb. 11, 2024).

paper.[3] In his later thesis, "The Vulnerable World Hypothesis," Bostrom uses logic to show that in a world of escalating biological, technological, and even ideological advances, human ideas such as regional democracy and freedom from surveillance will become irrelevant. He describes his paper as being a "risk-benefit balance of developments towards ubiquitous surveillance or a unipolar world order." This is to be understood as an allegorical, perhaps even satirical argument — one that nonetheless describes very real problems. As Bostrom's abstract states:

> Scientific and technological progress might change people's capabilities or incentives in ways that would destabilize civilization. For example, advances in DIY biohacking tools might make it easy for anybody with basic training in biology to kill millions; novel military technologies could trigger arms races in which whoever strikes first has a decisive advantage; or some economically advantageous process may be invented that produces disastrous negative global externalities that are hard to regulate.[4]

Rather than advocating for a one-world government and total surveillance of the human population to prevent and mitigate risks, Bostrom's paper instead seeks to show that the fabric of our societies, and the substance of our inventions, make the alternatives

---

3   Nick Bostrom, "The Simulation Argument," *Philosophical Quarterly*, 2003, Vol. 53, No. 211, p243-255.

4   Nick Bostrom, "The Vulnerable World hypothesis," *Global Policy*, Vol. 10, Issue 4, 2019, https://nickbostrom.com/papers/vulnerable.pdf (Accessed Feb. 11, 2024).

to totalitarianism a worse bet than authoritarian control, statistically speaking. The freedom we experience as a result of access to technology — most of which is borne from development budgets for military application — brings with it a new set of risks. Many believe those risks to be so great, that any strategy we pursue to mitigate them could itself pose an existential threat to the values of democracy and human freedom. This is the type of contradiction Bostrom's paper seeks to explore.

One of many among these new technological risks is the possibility that remote-operated drones — which have been a staple of Western foreign policy, long used for strategic, state-sanctioned murder[5] — become as lethal, ubiquitous, and difficult to regulate as the USA's current firearms market. The intersection of technologies such as facial recognition, systems hacking, and the increasing availability and decreasing size of drones means they could become a severe threat to life, as George Dvorsky writes:

> Scenarios include the deliberate crashing of multiple self-driving vehicles, coordinated attacks using thousands of micro-drones, converting commercial drones into face-recognizing assassins, and holding critical infrastructures for ransom.[6]

---

5   The data around state-sanctioned military drone strikes is hard to parse, and split across studies and reports with different methodologies — a study of drone missions carried out by UK forces conducted by dronewars. net (https://dronewars.net/uk-drone-strike-list-2) from freedom of information requests lists specific data for the number of missions, but does not specify total casualties. (Accessed Feb. 11, 2024).

6   George Dvorsky, "New Report on Emerging AI Risks Paints a Grim Future," *Gizmodo*, Feb. 21, 2018, https://gizmodo.com/new-report-on-ai-risks-paints-a-grim-future-1823191087 (Accessed Feb. 11, 2024).

Just as John Barnes presciently predicted in *Kaleidoscope Century*, these technologies can become more deadly as they begin to intersect. This is, of course, even further complicated when the operators of remote drones are no longer human — a scenario that is already fast approaching, as Frank Pasquale writes:

> At present, the military-industrial complex is speeding us toward the development of drone swarms that operate independently of humans, ostensibly because only machines will be fast enough to anticipate the enemy's counter-strategies. This is a self-fulfilling prophecy, tending to spur an enemy's development of the very technology that supposedly justifies militarisation of algorithms.[7]

Pasquale argues against the "reformist discourse of imparting ethics to military robots" as a pipe dream, but as his article states, the coming of both micro-drone technology in military contexts, and the likelihood that human pilots will one day no longer be required, are both pretty much assured. Even Naomi Klein, who has written extensively about the potentially disastrous effects of technologically-accelerated hypercapitalism, still falls into the trap of talking about these developments as part of a "future" that could be avoided if people just mustered the will to slow down, to stop, and think:

---

7   Frank Pasquale, "Machines Set Loose to Slaughter," *The Guardian*, Oct. 15, 2020, https://www.theguardian.com/news/2020/oct/15/danger-ous-rise-of-military-ai-drone-swarm-autonomous-weapons (Accessed Feb. 11, 2024).

... in the future that is hastily being constructed, all of these trends are poised for a warp-speed acceleration. [...] It's a future that claims to be run on "artificial intelligence," but is actually held together by tens of millions of anonymous workers tucked away in warehouses, data centers, content-moderation mills, electronic sweatshops, lithium mines, industrial farms, meat-processing plants and prisons, where they are left unprotected from disease and hyper-exploitation. It's a future in which our every move, our every word, our every relationship is trackable, traceable and data-mineable by unprecedented collaborations between government and tech giants.[8]

The future Klein describes is already here. The likelihood that advanced artificial intelligence, even if it could and did achieve sentience, would change the state of play with regards to how populations are exploited and surveilled is almost nil, because these technologies will reflect the values and worldviews of their designers. Today, they are in service to extractivist capitalism. They mine us for data, they influence us to consume. There is little reason to assume that this will change, or at least not in favor of returning rights and privacy to citizens. The loss of these rights is almost never discussed; the loss of privacy is accepted as a necessary cost of technological progress. Notions of "privacy" online are bunk when hacking is so prevalent, and the capture of

---

8   Naomi Klein, "How Big Tech Plans to Profit from the Pandemic," *The Guardian*, May 13, 2020, https://www.theguardian.com/news/2020/may/13/naomi-klein-how-big-tech-plans-to-profit-from-coronavirus-pandemic (Accessed Feb. 11, 2024).

data universal. They already have our information. As the technology writer Cory Doctorow points out: "Making it possible for the state to open your locks in secret means that anyone who works for the state, or anyone who can bribe or coerce anyone who works for the state, can have the run of your life."[9] Here, Doctorow was specifically referring to encryption in messaging apps and governmental attempts to go around it, but the same logic applies to any data that any given corporate or government entity holds on an individual. The site of our most intense surveillance, for now, is on our mobile phones. But mobiles are far from the first "monitoring device" we have taken to the heart of the capitalist imaginary. If anything, the mobile phone can perhaps best be understood as a conduit, connecting you "in real time" to the vagaries and trends of the bustling "free market," as the writer and sociologist William Davies writes:

> Understood as real-time monitoring devices, markets are not so much tools for processing facts but for gauging our feelings. This is where faith in the market maps onto populism and nationalism, for all those creeds see politics as little other than mass public coordination via shared feeling. Reason becomes sidelined in favour of sentiment.[10]

Davies' analogy of the market-as-monitoring device speaks to the very foundations of neoliberal theory and free market belief

---

9   Cory Doctorow, "Theresa May Wants to Ban Crypto," *Boing Boing*, Jun. 4, 2017, https://boingboing.net/2017/06/04/theresa-may-king-canute.html (Accessed Feb. 11, 2024).

10 William Davies, *Nervous States* (W.W. Norton & Co., 2018), p167.

systems. It is the embodiment of the post-Foucault "control society" described by Gilles Deleuze and Felix Guattari, and later Byung-Chul Han. This system seeks to impose its will not through ideological argument and oppression, but by surveillance, prediction, and oblique influence. Byung-Chul Han writes: "The smartphone is not an object but an infomat, or even an informant, monitoring and influencing us."[11]

The story of the Cambridge Analytica scandal demonstrates how that "influence" plays out in our real lives. It is the story of Russian interference in US elections; Russian dark money in Westminster. The story of Chinese "social credit" systems, and the capture of our discourse by algorithmic distortions. Most of all it is the story of "micro-targeting" — how our personal data has been collected, weaponized, and then leveraged against us. As investigative journalist Carole Cadwalladr, who broke the Cambridge Analytica scandal, writes: "This is not just a story about social psychology and data analytics. It has to be understood in terms of a military contractor using military strategies on a civilian population. Us."[12]

The use of digital technologies, and the belief that they are at once benign, or have the power to improve our lives, is dependent upon our acceptance that we will be both monitored and influenced. In that sense, Byung Chul-Han's argument[13] that we are

---

11 Byung-Chul Han: "I Practise Philosophy as Art," *ArtReview*, Dec. 2, 2021, https://artreview.com/byung-chul-han-i-practise-philosophy-as-art (Accessed Feb. 11, 2024).

12 Carole Cadwalladr, "The Great British Brexit Robbery," *The Guardian*, May 7, 2017, https://www.theguardian.com/technology/2017/may/07/ the-great-british-brexit-robbery-hijacked-democracy (Accessed Feb. 11, 2024).

13 Drawing on Michel Foucault's *Discipline and Punish* (Pantheon Books,

subjects of a digital panopticon is absolutely accurate. The whole method of algorithmic influence, and the data capture that makes it possible, is premised on the idea that human thought can be identified, measured, and quantified. As William Davies argues, the belief in technology's ability to understand human nature: "rests on the idea that 'thoughts' are nothing but a series of physical motions, whose patterns can be easily read like the smile on a face or an encrypted message to be hacked. What things really *mean* is ultimately just a question of pattern recognition… In that sense, *all* interpretation and understanding is akin to code breaking."[14] Our submission to surveillance is masked by the illusion that smartphones give us control, as Davies continues: "The allure of the smartphone derives from its military inheritance: the screen represents a world that is obedient to our commands… [Apps and devices] offer us the chance to exercise small acts of dominance ourselves, over taxi drivers, information, and material goods."[15]

This promise of control finds a weird echo in the paranoid fantasies of those who claim to have experienced the phenomenon known as "gang stalking." Gang stalking subjects come to believe that they are being surveilled in the real world by strangers, and sometimes friends and family. The belief that "gang stalking" exists is reinforced by online communities that share stories of shadowy figures by whom they are pursued and persecuted. Frequently these pursuers are imagined as government agents, representatives of a shadow state. In common with the

---

1977), Byung Chul-Han makes the argument that we live in a digital panopticon in *Psychopolitics: Neoliberalism and New Technologies of Power* (Verso Books, 2014).

14 Davies, *Nervous States*, p181.

15 Davies, *Nervous States*, p186-187.

vast majority of conspiracy narratives, the person subject to gang stalking is the focus of elaborate, malign intentions. They are pursued and harassed because of "what they know." In much the same way, we are surveilled to find out what *we* know and believe so that the free market can rush in and fulfill our desires (hopefully, desires that carefully match the ones capitalism sought to create in the first place). As Jean Guerrero writes for *Wired*, discussing her father's descent into "gang stalking" communities online:

> In our digital economy, covert players are constantly harvesting our data and churning out exquisitely tuned consumer profiles to tap into our dreams and desires. We are being surveilled. We are being controlled and manipulated. We are perhaps being tortured. But it's not the CIA or aliens perpetrating all this. We are doing it to ourselves.[16]

Guerrero's father, who believed he was subject to surveillance and control by nefarious, shadowy US government forces, was a crank and a crazy man when he was alone with his delusions. When he discovered the concept of "gang stalking" he instantly became transfigured, in his own imagination, into a symbol — a member of a "community" of "targeted individuals." As Guerrero writes: "This is the promise made by the digital realm: that if we surrender our minds to it, if we prize it above the people we love, we will be rewarded with a kind of immortality." We will be recognized and validated if we categorize ourselves. If we obey.

---

16 Jean Guerrero, "My Father Says He's a 'Targeted Individual.' Maybe We All Are," *Wired*, Oct. 25, 2018, https://www.wired.com/story/my-father-says-hes-a-targeted-individual-maybe-we-all-are (Accessed Feb. 11, 2024).

This all hinges on our conception of ourselves, our belief we are each the "main characters" of our lives. It's a conception reinforced with ever-greater emphasis by consumer capitalism. The most obvious example of this can be found in video games, specifically the genre of the "first person shooter." Whether the player engages in combat with virtual zombies or real, online "avatars," these games completely embody the solipsism of our self-image as capitalist subjects and consumers, as Yussuf Cole writes:

> When you play *Black Ops*, the only parts of the country you see are shadowy government representatives and disembodied voices on the other side of a two-way mirror. The only civilians you meet are the corporate goons who soak up government contracts in order to build you bigger exosuits to die in… This insularity, this conversation only within self, has dire ideological consequences.[17]

Cole is right to identify a nihilistic reading of ideology and politics in games like *Call of Duty*, which use real-world populations and communities as the basis of their "othered" (killable) non-player characters. But the same is true of any game where you (the subject) play the hero, and everyone else is a target or collateral. These games reproduce the idea of the self as "the chosen one" — the subject who sees through all ideologies, the subject meant to redeem through sacrifice and struggle. Any discussion of the first-person shooter is a discussion about whether we see

---

17 Yussef Cole, "The Hollow Nihilism of Call of Duty," *Wired*, 2020, https://www.wired.com/story/call-of-duty-black-ops-history (Accessed Feb. 11, 2024).

ourselves as heroes or villains. Villains, of course, represent "ideology" while the hero is codified as "non-ideological."

The 1999 cyberpunk film *The Matrix* is the ur-text of this discourse in the current era. Derived from the aesthetics and subject matter of William Gibson's *Neuromancer*,[18] its influence and importance as a symbolic system is evident in the appropriation of the original film's "red pill / blue pill" allegory by the "men's rights" movement. So-called "incels" refer to their radicalization as being "blackpilled." Inevitably, the suffix "-pilled" can now be applied across any political axis — it is simply shorthand for the idea of illumination, of waking from illusion. As with many metaphors, the synonym implies the antonym. To take a "pill" from any ideology is to "wake up" into a new reality, based on new assumptions and limitations. From the point of view of such an awakening, the reality on the other side of the glass is the false one. There can never be a synthesis of the two.

It is telling that the *Matrix* movies involve a narrative that pits "agents" against "subjects" — the agents are programs intended to enforce compliance with false reality; the subjects are the enslaved, disembodied consciousnesses of the "real" protagonists. The implication here is that to "awaken" is to find agency — to become an agent, to escape the prison of the subject. Behind this is the implication that once awakened, we will find kindred souls, much like the community of the stalked found by Jean Guerrero's father. Perhaps this is the secret of *The Matrix* as a persistent cultural symbol — we are all surveilled and pursued by agents. We are all the sleeper, the subject who must awaken.[19]

---

18 William Gibson, *Neuromancer* (Ace, 1984).
19 A Jewish friend pointed out to me that the phrase "The Sleeper must awaken," taken from Frank Herbert's 1965 spiritual space opera classic

Awakening always carries the charge of religious epiphany. In 1974, the science fiction writer Phillip K. Dick experienced a vision in which a whole belief system and alternative history of the world was "revealed" to him, along with a new understanding of time. In Dick's visions, and their accompanying theology (which is unpacked in his posthumously-published *Exegesis*[20]), the Roman Empire never ended. Our time was merely a hallucinatory pseudo-reality, a simulation designed to ensure control by hegemonic Roman powers. Dick became aware of a protective entity or entities that takes our "side" against this domination — the consciousness he came to describe as V.A.L.I.S. (Vast Active Living Intelligence System). His devotion to decoding and explaining this epiphany, which included a new understanding of Christian theology, occupied Dick until his death. The complexity and absurdity of his theological "system" serve only to conceal its utility as one among many meticulous clockwork allegories for coercion and social control in the author's canon; another signifier of whose "real" is the true reality. His own obsession with the "reality" of, and evidence for this system is like Guerrero's father's descent into the "real" of a conspiracy community. It is not a fiction or an allegory, to the subject. The simulation, the shared delusion, is

---

Dune (Chilton Books, 1965), is likely based on a verse from the "Shofar" prayer offered at the Jewish New Year: "Awake, ye sleepers from your slumber, and rouse you from your lethargy. Scrutinise your deeds and return in repentance." (Sourced from Jewish Ideas Daily: http://www.jewishideas-daily.com/5000/features/the-shofar, accessed Feb. 11, 2024). This parallel demonstrates the ontology of "awakening" as a legacy of a specifically Judaeo-Christian thought-system, and another that would qualify as a "secular heresy" by John Gray's definition, outlined in chapter 2.

20 Philip K. Dick (Ed. Pamela Jackson, Jonathan Lethem), *The Exegesis of Phillip K. Dick* (Houghton Mifflin Harcourt, 2011).

experienced as "reality" itself. This is an echo of tl
liam Gibson would give for cyberspace, a term he
an oft-cited passage from *Neuromancer*, he des‹
space we occupy online as a "consensual hallucination."

Like Dick, in the world of *The Matrix*, Neo awakens into a world with a new historicism, a new timeline; chosen from the "unreal" prison reality as a subject with the power to escape, to awaken from it. He is the subject to whom agency is revealed — both as enforced control (the "agents" who come to eliminate him, to prevent his awakening), and "liberating" control, through the revelation that he has agency, and can control his destiny ("I know kung fu…"). The allegory at play in *The Matrix* implies that Neo has reached the reality beyond the simulation when he awakens on the Nebuchadnezzar (a "base" craft used by the film's principal characters). But within this reality, he is still framed as the hero, the archetype — the (Chosen) One. The revealed system — the hidden city of Babylon, the war with the machines, offers no more empirical evidence of its objective truth than the simulation itself.

If there were a science fiction film capable of representing the "real" of ideology in action — the true, bleak and brutal reality of capitalist exploitation and imperial extractivism — it would not be found in the simplistic imagery of *The Matrix*, with its H.R. Giger-esque, egg-sac battery farm containers. This is just another shallow visual metaphor that asks you to awaken from one cap-italist hero-story into another. Such a film might bear closer resemblance to 2013's bleak Russian take on the genre, *Hard to be a God*, in which scientific members of a space-faring Earth culture become involved in the horror of another planet's feudal conflicts. Both interference and non-interference in the feudal culture — their attempts to influence and "improve" it, and their submission to it, their exploitation of it — reach the same terminus. Piles of corpses. In the film's schema, there would have been no possible way to "awaken" the medieval subjects of the backwards planet. The so-called "advances" of the Earthers' technological society reflect the same inequalities, the same methods of coercion and control. Whether the participants are "awakened" or not is immaterial. In most cases, both sides will assume they are awakened, while the other side is deceived. Whichever version wins out as truth, and whichever is deemed heresy, the victors will nearly always triumph in bloodshed, chaos, and destruction. The reality to which one awakens or from which one wishes to awaken is the reality of the victor. The African proverb about lions and historians, popularised in the 1990s by poet and novelist Chinua Achebe, forever holds true: "Until the lions have their own historians, the history of the hunt will always glorify the hunter." To wish for awakening is to dream of alternate realities — to create, within oneself, a simulation.

To "awaken" does not guarantee that we have not entered another simulation, another false consciousness — this much is implied by Nick Bostrom's "Simulation Argument" paper, first published online in 2001, two years after the original *Matrix* movie dominated the summer box office. Bostrom writes that our inability to perceive whether or not we live in an "ancestor simulation" implies the existence of a "basement level" of reality — the final reality, beneath all of the layers of nested simulations, where the first ancestor simulation was created. Just as any political, personal, or spiritual awakening seems to reveal to us a pre-existing pattern or truth, the awakening from one level of a simulation into another does not prove that one has reached the basement. None of our political realities have any more solid ground than these simulated "levels" of a Bostrom reality stack. In just the same way, we cannot prove the reality or non-reality of our subjective experience by codifying it. If our lives are shaped by ideologies, then we must be able to traverse them, to move between them — otherwise the argument is simply one of whose subjective reality is the most "real," with no proof possible.

As yet, we understand little about the capabilities, intentions, and evolution of artificial intelligences, despite the advances these creations have made in the past decade. The use of algorithms — in essence, a limited form of artificial intelligence themselves — to shape not just our media landscape, but our democratic norms and social codes is an experiment with no clear intent besides profit and control. This is the aspect of surveillance culture that is under-appreciated — we do not know what algorithms do with our data. That world is concealed beneath an opaque layer of copyrighted code, behind intellectual property laws. Artificial intelligences are already accessing, learning from, and simulating our thoughts, speech and behaviors based on our online data. As multiple studies show, the AIs that result from this learning process often reflect the biases, prejudices and general unpleasantness of the data they have captured. All of our rage, our bile, our hatred — this is what the machines read when they survey our code. The recent craze for feeding keywords or images into AIs like Dall-E Mini or Midjourney to produce randomly generated AI "art" may be diverting. But just as the Cambridge Analytica scandal revealed how early internet "personality quizzes" on Facebook and other platforms were used to capture location data, browsing habits and other demographic information from users, only for it to be sold on for profit and leverage to private companies and political parties, we do not know what the insights our image requests and online "chats" with AIs will generate, in terms of surplus data. Will it be leveraged, like the Cambridge Analytica data, by shadowy corporate interests? Or instead, are we effectively singing songs to the infant versions of a species we have designed to replace us? What does an artificial intelligence dream of when we ask it to paint Taylor Swift in a Korean karaoke bar in the style of Pablo Picasso? What does that tell the machines about us?

In a very real sense, the machines are already our replacements. Machine learning research tends to focus on replicating human capacities, usually so they can be massified and outsourced. This is not solely confined to robots replacing factory workers. Artificial intelligences can now replace writers, with dire consequences for the fields of journalism and truth-telling, as Jonathan Haidt writes:

> Artificial intelligence is close to enabling the limitless spread of highly believable disinformation. The AI program GPT-3 is already so good that you can give it a topic and a tone and it will spit out as many essays as you like, typically with perfect grammar and a surprising level of coherence. In a year or two, when the program is upgraded to GPT-4, it will become far more capable.[21]

The weaponization of text-generating artificial intelligence is not just a threat to the very concept of journalism as a career and a discipline, but a threat to the ethics of that discipline, and to

---

21 Jonathan Haidt, "Why the Past Ten Years of American Life Have Been Uniquely Stupid," *The Atlantic*, Apr. 11, 2022, https://www.theatlantic.com/magazine/archive/2022/05/social-media-democracy-trust-babel/629369 (Accessed Feb. 11, 2024).

truth-telling as a societal pillar. In a world where machine intelligences can create multiple conflicting narratives and realities
around us, how do we know which pill to take, which world to
wake up from, and which into? By building machines who can
talk, think, and write for us, have we already obscured our own
speech, thought, and writing? Are we building artificial intelligences, or are they learning from us? We can program as many
failsafes into machine learning systems as we want. There will
always be someone who can reverse-engineer those restrictions
and remove or modify them. Weaponization is inherent in invention; most technologies we use in the home are forms of modified
military hardware.

Reality is all too easily weaponized, because all it takes to
"wake up" from it is for someone to convince you that you were
"asleep." In truth, your beliefs, your worldview, your opinions and
your culture were always in some sense fabricated for you — by
your family, your social group, the era you were born in, the influences you were exposed to. A challenge to these preset variables
can be experienced as an attack, something that destabilizes the
way you think about gender, or race, or class, or any other number of topics about which you may have made assumptions; about
which you may possess biases and prejudices. That challenge can
also be experienced as the revelation of a truth, or a pattern, that
was hitherto unseen. Though we perhaps cannot help but view
the world through this lens of revelation or destruction, we must
distrust both instincts. There is no other "reality" to wake up into.
That too is a secular heresy, just like the digital hereafter promised by the transhumanists, or the neoliberal vision of interstellar
post-scarcity. Both are versions of the Christian heaven. They are
false promises, offered to slaves. There is nothing to which we,

as individuals or as a society, can ascend. We may have already passed the peak. Imagined, alternative states of "freedom" mask the cage we all live in — the contours of our reality, where conformity and compulsion are marketed as "choice." As Žižek says: "The true problem of freedom today is precisely unfreedom which is experienced as freedom."[22] Perhaps it is time to stop imagining alternate worlds, and confront whatever monsters are lurking in the basement.

---

22 Slavoj Žižek, "For a Left That Dares To Speak Its Name," Institute for the Radical Imagination, Oct. 8, 2019, https://youtu.be/qxz4zkO_ce4 (Accessed Feb. 11, 2024).

six

TYPE ZERO KARDASHEV

When we are headed the wrong way, the last thing we
need is progress.[1]

—Nick Bostrom

Designed by Joshua Lengfelder and launched in 2020 with
help from cofounder Auburn Salcedo, *Randonautica*[2] is
described by its creator as "the world's first quantumly generated
reality game."[3] A random number generator gives the player a set
of real-world coordinates. The player sets out to reach that destination, and sees what happens. Dedicated "randonauts" will
follow strings of coordinates, and often report strange coincidences, bizarre sights, or frightening mysteries. Destinations can
be set within a localized area, meaning that even a randonaut with

---

1   Nick Bostrom, "Genetic Enhancement and the Future of Humanity,"
     The European Magazine, 2011, archived at https://web.archive.org/
     web/20181231163914/https://www.theeuropean-magazine.com/nick-
     bostrom--2/6028-genetic-enhancement-and-the-future-of-humanity
     (Accessed Feb. 12, 2024).
2   Coincidentally, it launched in February of that year — the same month
     that Covid-19 officially hit the UK. The viral popularity of the game
     coinciding with lockdowns perhaps offers an explanation for its success.
     Many people were keen to get out of their house, but avoid human contact,
     although the Covid-19 lockdown did impose limitations in some jurisdic-
     tions on the length of journeys made outside the home.
3   The game's website gives an overview of its mechanics, its development,
     and the vision of Lengfelder's design: https://www.randonautica.com
     (Accessed Feb. 11, 2024).

limited resources for travel can still explore parts of their environment they might otherwise never reach, or encounter the familiar in strange circumstances. *Randonautica* is very similar to the augmented reality game *Pokemon Go*, but its aims and player rewards are much stranger.

The theory behind *Randonautica* is explained in more detail in the documents of the Fatum Project,[4] which details Lengfelder and his colleagues' hypothesis that consciousness *creates* reality, rather than consciousness being a *product* of reality. This represents a radical inversion of traditional non-dualistic beliefs, which see human consciousness as part of a spectrum that includes all living things in a unified field. This thinking is backed up by in-depth conceptual research into quantum physics, but the Fatum Project's hypothesis also offers weird echoes of Nick Bostrom's "Simulation Argument"[5] paper. By sending players to random locations and encouraging them to notice patterns, coincidences and mysteries (the game's website simply calls these "adventures"), *Randonautica* could be seen as pushing at the boundaries of what can be simulated; how much processing power the simulation, if it is a simulation, can draw upon. Looked at through the prism of Bostrom's argument (as outlined in the previous chapter), Randonauts could be seen to be testing the limits of the in-world data processing of the ancestor simulation we may have mistaken for "the real world," by focusing on areas that are often (or are supposed to remain) unexplored. Back alleys, wheat fields, deserted lots, abandoned shopping malls — the Fatum Project calls these "blindspots". It is here that some

---

4   The Fatum Project's mission statement can be read at https://www.randonautica.com/theory (Accessed Feb. 11, 2024).

5   Nick Bostrom, "The Simulation Argument," *Philosophical Quarterly*, 2003, Vol. 53, No. 211, p243-255.

randonauts report that they can see the careless repetition of simple base codes; they can detect the shading on the polygons, see the gaps in the clouds.

The content of randonaut adventures can be "set" by the player, who projects their "intention" when generating the random destination. This has echoes of the aims and techniques of chaos magick, with its manipulation of semiotic signs and symbols to drive intent, and in the psychedelic field guides of 1960s pioneers like Timothy Leary which emphasize the importance of "set and setting" in a therapeutic context when using LSD or psilocybin. By implication, a *Randonautica* player who selects carelessly (or indeed randomly) might leave themselves open to a negative or frightening encounter (a "bad trip," to use the language of psychedelics). This would appear to be very similar to the logical schema of self-help books like multi-million bestseller *The Secret*,[6] which encourages the reader to project their intention or will into the world in order to see their dreams realized. To fail to do this is, by implication, to languish; to be a subject of capitalism, a pawn of fate and not an agent of destiny, and therefore capital. It is to accept that one is perhaps a "non-player character" and an unimportant piece of furniture in the ancestor simulation, rather than an awakened mind. It is also the reflection of the paranoid fantasy which places the self at the center of some vast and frightening conspiracy, where each shadow or glance is interpreted as threat or malice. Such a world can be populated only by those who see themselves as being forced into the role of powerless NPCs, or heroic pariahs gang-stalked by malign, non-human Agents at every turn.

---

6   Rhonda Byrne, *The Secret* (Atria Books / Beyond Worlds Publishing, 2006).

Perhaps the appeal of *Randonautica* is less about showing us the bars of the cage that is the proposed ancestor simulation we inhabit; less about finding oneself aligned with the will, caprice, or intent of the universe; and more about abrogating oneself to the machine gaze. The sense of a story, the hints of a hidden or wider world that *Randonautica* adventures can bring to the player all depend upon the very real phenomenon of pareidolia — the tendency for the human eye and brain to interpret patterns in incoming data. The same instinct that leads us to see forgotten carvings and fallen temples in Martian landscapes is the one which leads randonauts on their adventures, whether they find the happy coincidence of true love, or end up witnessing some unspeakable act of violence.[7] YouTube is full of videos of randonauts warning others not to use the game, for every reason you could imagine — from the fact it offers proof of the "Simulation Argument" or the "Mandela Effect," to accusations of Satanism, "deep state" manipulation, or the rise of malign machine intelligences. The Reddit thread dedicated to *Randonautica*[8] contains some eye-popping accounts, but like most of Reddit, it probably shares a lot of DNA with early "creepypasta" threads and forums, which involve clearly fabricated "real-life" horror stories. Above all else, *Randonautica* is a storytelling engine, one which lends itself to creepypasta-inspired horror of the kind Nick Antosca explored in his terrific TV series *Channel Zero*.

---

7   A 2020 *Vice* article (https://www.vice.com/en/article/bv8dk4/jamie-lee-curtis-taete-randonaut-photos, accessed Feb. 11, 2024) offers an account of what a *Randonautica* adventure feels like.

8   *Randonautica* on Reddit: https://www.reddit.com/r/Randonautica (accessed Feb. 11, 2024).

However, such divergences say little about the wider implications of *Randonautica*. Its coordinates are generated using quantum randomness; in theory the same weave of pattern and chaos which drives each moment of our unchosen lives. This begs the question behind Bostrom's argument. Are the patterns we see evidence of intent, of design? Are they evidence of artifice, of unreality? How can we tell?

Randonautica might tell us about the inherent storytelling nature of our consciousness, our memories and our culture. It also speaks to the emergence of artificial intelligence. If randonauts are using machine-generated numbers to send them to real-world coordinates, what do the machines who crunch the data learn from the interaction? How is that data leveraged? *Randonautica* represents the polar opposite of the fervently-anticipated "next wave" of communications technology — augmented reality, and virtual worlds. In an AR adventure, signs, advertisements, NPCs, and special effects may be overlaid across real-world environments, transforming reality into a liminal space between the metaverse and meat-space. This technology, as it accelerates and proliferates, will also follow the logic and algorithms of *Pokemon Go*, gamifying and corporatizing public and private space in ways we are yet to fully imagine. The metaverse is conceived as an escape from reality, a plane where anything is possible, and where anyone can be anything they want. The data gathered by players of such apps could no doubt be manipulated to work in the opposite direction. An artificial intelligence with access to that data could effectively use the processing power and storytelling abilities of human brains to map and configure the territory of the real. There is a commonplace in social media discourse — if you're not the customer, you're the product. In the same way, users of

Randonautica, who follow machine maps and report back telemetry to the emergent techno-intelligences of the internet, might well be generating data that could in some way transform or alter the curve of machine learning. This could include laying the technological foundations for the creation of ancestor simulations.

It could be argued that Bostrom's hypothesis is characteristic of the ideas a society generates when it is entering its endgame. Like the fictions of Philip K. Dick, Bostrom's paper asks us to consider whether our reality is real. By doing so, it also asks us whether any of this matters — if this is just a game, why save the ecosystem? Why hold down a job or put effort into maintaining relationships if the construct into which we invest is mere illusion? There's a vain hope in there, too, of some salvation from humankind's dark, apocalyptic fate — simulations can be hacked, artificial realities can be re-programmed much more easily than environmental devastation can be reversed. To question whether the world one lives in is truly real is also to ask whether one is responsible for it, or whether one is simply the dupe of another, who knows more. Ancestor simulation technology may find echoes in contemporary science fiction and the design of "games" like *Randonautica*, but the processing power required to run an ancestor simulation as complex as the world we live in, even for one player, would be astronomical.

In 1964, the Soviet astronomer Nikolai Kardashev put forward a theory for measuring the technological advancement of civilizations, from the global to the intergalactic. His model became known as the Kardashev Scale. One of its principal metrics is energy output and consumption. In Kardashev's framework, the highest level of civilization is a Type III — such a culture would be able to harness and use the power of each star in its galaxy as they wished, perhaps using a theorized techno-material called "computronium."[9] Such a material — a substrate that can absorb and process energy, convert its state, and broadcast it to where it needs to go — could be used to construct "Dyson spheres"[10] to harness galactic stellar energy in its entirety.

Even a Type II civilization, which can draw upon the resources of the star in its native system, might be able to produce a convincing ancestor simulation. Writers can (and have) imagined the deployment of such a simulation in response to nuclear war or ecological disaster as a way to save humanity from its downfall. This has echoes in the voluntary transhumanist "heaven" of uploaded consciousnesses. Going by Kardashev's logic, humanity's arrival as a Type II culture may occur in the next century or two (this is correct according to the physicist Michio Kaku and others). To reach such a level, we would need to be able to harness all of the energy our star outputs (but not yet all that it generates). As of yet, we have not weaned ourselves from fossil fuels mined from the Earth — we are nowhere near a Type I civilization.

This implies a solution to another theory of science and civilization — the paradox outlined by Enrico Fermi, which points at the glaring contradiction between the statistical probability of life emerging on other planets, and the complete lack of evidence for its emergence. Many have applied this paradox to come to a very dark conclusion about Kardashev's planetary "types." Perhaps there are no Type II civilizations; perhaps no Type I's

---

9   Computronium is a theorised form of programmable matter proposed by
     Norman Margolus and Tommaso Toffoli of MIT in 1991.
10   A Dyson sphere is a theoretical interstellar superstructure for capturing
     stellar energy, proposed in 1960 by Freeman Dyson, but also theorised in
     Olaf Stapleton's classic science fiction novel *Star Maker* (Methuen, 1937).

either. Perhaps all cultures poison or exterminate themselves, or are wiped out by chance or circumstance before they can reach the stars, or even adequately feed and clothe the starving millions on whose backs their progress is built. Perhaps all advanced civilizations flee into ancestor simulations as their physical worlds collapse or disappear, as Bostrom also speculates. In these solutions, there is no "darkest timeline" from which to flee. The silence that echoes back at us from the vast depths of space is all the evidence we need that our problems on Earth do not have solutions.

"The sun will survive 6 billion more years before its fuel runs out. And the expanding universe will continue far longer, perhaps forever,"[11] writes astrophysicist Martin Rees. He proposes that we embrace the pioneering ambitions of billionaire space travel enthusiasts such as Elon Musk and Richard Branson because we have time enough to escape the darker implications of Fermi's challenge. Rees' view is the classic techno-utopian one where the emerging hybridity of human and machine will deliver progress, while all cultural and historical obstacles to the unification of mankind in the singular goal of galactic expansion and exploration will simply melt away into egalitarianism. He confidently continues:

> ... [Even] if intelligent life had originated only on the Earth, it need not remain a trivial feature of the cosmos: it could jump-start a diaspora whereby ever more complex intelligence spreads through the whole galaxy, via self-reproducing machines, transmitting

---

11   Martin Rees, "NASA's Webb Telescope is a Joy. But it's the Private Ventures That Push at its Limits," *The Guardian*, Jan. 2, 2022, https://www.theguardian.com/commentisfree/2022/jan/02/james-webb-space-telescope-thrilling-future-for-mankind, (Accessed Feb. 11, 2024).

DNA, instructions for 3D printers or suchlike. Interstellar voyages would hold no terrors for near-immortals. There's plenty of time ahead.

To describe a diaspora of benign, near-immortal techno-augmented beings from the broken shell of a planet ruined by their extractivism is yet another Christian heresy. It is a vision of the faithful being lifted up from chaos and apocalypse into pure transcendence. It is the kind of promise you would only make if you knew the person you promised it to was already doomed: "Yes, there's a better world coming. Soon you will be there, and all your troubles soothed." For all that this promise is spoken in terms of human-machine merger and scientific discovery, it is still a fantasy of transcendence, and not an account of how reality actually proceeds. Time has no arrow from the present to the future, or at least not one that travels in a straight line. That perceived line of flight arises from a trick of the human eye due to our short lifespans. Progress, if it can be spoken of at all, is fractured, fragmented, and most of all, incremental and fragile. Technologies, wisdom, and even the stories we have spun can all be lost and erased, never to be recreated. This is the heart of Fermi's dilemma. The advanced alien species we like to imagine — do they sit and laugh at us from the cosmic sidelines? Perhaps there is a galactic "police force" of some kind that wipes out problematic civilizations, sterilizing their planets. Perhaps a capricious, ancient species will return to cull us, Thanos-style, as soon as Vladimir Putin or Joe Biden reach for the red button. All these scenarios seem too convenient. If aliens do exist, is it not just as likely that they are dead? Are we doomed to their fate, destined to find only ruins when we reach their distant planets?

Even such questions betray a hubristic anthropomorphism. Nobody reaches anywhere, all our planets are dead. Even if we encountered alien life, or it encountered us, we might not see each other as "alive." Alien species might be "conscious" in ways we cannot comprehend. We barely understand the consciousness of the creatures with whom we share a planet. We are simply part of a biome, insignificant in the vastness of space; cut off from anything that might resemble us except the creatures we slaughter for food and profit, or through our carelessness.

In that sense, we are all randonauts. We follow pre-programmed vectors, the mathematics of which are completely inscrutable to us. The data we capture goes nowhere, in the vast context of galactic time. Even if we were to find some recess where alien life exists, and transmit that data to them, it would likely mean nothing — just another pretty pattern, like our unique thumbprints, or the zone lines in the heart of the last tree.

seven

INFINITE VERSE

All your base are belong to us.[1]
> —Text of a meme based on the
> 1991 Sega Megadrive game *Zero Wing*

Mark Zuckerberg and Elon Musk are self-styled billionaire-kings of an internet based on extractivist data-mining, malign surveillance and algorithmic manipulation. Zuckerberg wants to get in on the ground level of the emergent "metaverse" and stake it out as corporate territory on behalf of investors and advertisers. Musk meanwhile has his eye on corporate domination and monopoly, with his malfunctioning bid to co-opt and control the "public square" of Twitter discourse and create an all-encompassing "everything app" (under the stunningly imaginative name "X"). The social media business model is dying because it was always "free" to the user, but the social costs are ever more apparent. Twitter and Facebook require eyeballs. But people do not want to just watch, consume and broadcast online. They want to cooperate — to play; to talk, tell stories, and create. Musk, Zuckerberg and others plan to own the spaces where this happens.

The future of gaming is not necessarily about what players are prepared to spend, but where they want to spend time. The shared worlds of online gaming already offer obvious parallels with the

---

1   Source: https://knowyourmeme.com/memes/all-your-base-are-belong-to-us (Accessed Mar. 4, 2024).

emerging "'metaverse." Discord servers dedicated to *Minecraft*, *Roblox* and *Fortnite* are home to professional players, streaming creators and fans. These virtual spaces are busy and populated, in stark contrast to the mostly empty corporate hallways of Meta's fake plastic worlds, and less susceptible to the trolling that these blank, culture-free spaces invite. As the critic Mike Watson writes:

> The power relations of gaming need to be judged based on what is specific to interactions within gaming, on what it means to exercise choice while being entertained as part of a team as opposed to being passive and often solitary consumers. This, together with the enhanced potential for choice making within new media, should be celebrated and built upon so that the positive aspects of gaming and social media might be deployed as a challenge to negative social phenomena.[2]

Watson suggests that there is truly transformative potential in these communities as drivers of social change, arguing they can positively affect how we see ourselves and each other, and perhaps even how we approach solidarity. The same is true of the virtual worlds within the games themselves, and the radical potential and meaning that emerges from taking part in shared-world storytelling.

The beloved space simulator *No Man's Sky* poses deep, existential questions about human nature, our future, and the simulations we might build inside the nascent "metaverse." You play an astronaut. The ships you fly, trade and repair are straight from the designs of Syd Mead and Ralph McQuarrie. The game's expertly minimalist world-building draws as much inspiration

---

2   Mike Watson, *Can the Left Learn to Meme?* (Zer0 Books, 2019), p84.

from the fiction of Isaac Asimov, Arthur C. Clarke, Frank Herbert and Robert Heinlein as it does from the unforgettable period cover art of Chris Foss and the psychedelic science fiction comics of Jean Giraud, better known as Mœbius. It's a shared visual language known to all hardcore science fiction fans.

The *Alien* and original *Star Wars* movies are storytelling touchstones, not the over-explained lore-fests of their later sequels, prequels and reboots. *2001* and *2010*, *Interstellar* and *Ad Astra* all feel like they could have taken place within the infinite universe of *No Man's Sky* alongside all of the *Trek* and *Wars* movies, shows like *Babylon 5*, and Iain Banks' towering *Culture* series. Nevertheless, the game's science fiction concepts take root in the soil of hard science. In a sequence reminiscent of the opening of *The Martian*, you first awaken with no memories on a strange planet. Your exosuit is malfunctioning, and you have minutes to live. The atmospheric soundtrack by 65daysofstatic amplifies the game's immersive qualities. The term "math rock" describes perfectly how they created the soundscapes for *No Man's Sky* alongside Paul Weir.[3]

The game's creator Sean Murray has cited *Star Control II*, *Elite* and *Freespace* as key influences, but *No Man's Sky* is on a different scale. The vastness of the map is thrilling. Each warp brings you closer to your chosen destination. There's no up, down, left, right or forward in space — just out, ever farther; or in, towards the crushing gravity of the centre. Procedural generation was Murray's game-changing innovation. There are a possible 18,446,744,073,709,551,616 planets to visit. The

---

3   For more on the procedural generation involved in the game's soundtrack, read an interview with the band in *Wired*: https://www.wired.co.uk/article/no-mans-sky-65daysofstatic-interview (Accessed Feb. 18, 2024).

process of generating these worlds depends on the creation of a mathematical "seed" for each galaxy, as Murray explained to the *New Yorker*:

> Each star's number becomes a seed that defines its orbiting planets, and the planetary numbers are used as seeds to define the qualities of planetary terrain, atmosphere, and ecology. In this way, the system combines entropy and structure…[4]

The storytelling, and the game's design itself, offer further parallels to Nick Bostrom's "Simulation Argument." Nobody within the world of *No Man's Sky* knows for sure whether they are in a simulation, and they question it often. The game asks you to interrogate the nature of reality, but simultaneously feels very "real" as you top up fuel, dodge storms, escape pirates, or run from the robot space police known as "sentinels."

The massive and long-running space sim *Eve Online* also engages with lofty questions about reality, existence and human nature. The game took off in the era of early 2000s "LAN parties," later moving to online play. Now entering its second decade, it remains the most-played space-based MMORPG (Massively Multiplayer Online Role-Playing Game) of all time, with a registered user count of 9 million at its peak.[5] *No Man's Sky*, by

---

4   Sean Murray, quoted in Raffi Khatchadourian, "World Without End," *New Yorker Magazine*, 11 May, 2015, https://www.newyorker.com/magazine/2015/05/18/world-without-end-raffi-khatchadourian (Accessed Feb. 18, 2024).

5   Source: https://mmo-population.com/r/eve#:~:text=EVE%20Online%20is%20estimated%20to%20have%209%2C462%2C474%20total%20players%20or%20subscribers (Accessed Feb. 18, 2024).

contrast, peaked at 200,000 active online players,[6] but has since plateaued. The universe of *Eve* (as it is commonly abbreviated) happens in "real-time." The game's history is perhaps the largest collaboratively-created piece of fiction humankind has ever written. A "persistent world" sim, it started at a point in the game's galactic "history," and continued. It offers a ruthlessly capitalist vision of space and intergalactic cultures, based around the formation of corporations who ally with, subjugate or protect the economic interests of competing groups. A galactic war in *Eve Online* in 2020 cost nearly $1 million in player assets[7] — an event referred to as the "EveOnline apocalypse."[8] *Eve's* "single shard" is a concept not unlike the shared continuity of the Marvel Cinematic Universe. Hundreds of thousands of players have contributed to this shared canon, and caused *Endgame*-level climactic battles without the guidance of a writers room, traditional "missions," or any other form of narrative structure.

If *Eve* asks payers to imagine a world where humans have evolved to become a Type III Kardashev species inhabiting a galactic core of 7,800 warring star systems, *No Man's Sky* offers a stranger vision — a larger universe full of mysteries and anomalies, sparsely populated with just a handful of space-faring species who rarely interact. If the *No Man's Sky* online play mode known as "Nexus" is a little more like *Eve Online*, asking players to focus

---

6   Source: https://steamcharts.com/app/275850 (Accessed Feb. 18, 2024).

7   Neil "Larinda" Bond, "How EVE Online's Players Started a War That's Cost $700K," IGN, https://www.ign.com/articles/how-eve-onlines-players-started-a-war-thats-cost-700k (Accessed Feb. 18, 2024).

8   Simon Parkin, "Eve Online: How a Virtual World Went to the Edge of Apocalypse and Back," *The Guardian*, 12 May, 2015, https://www.theguardian.com/technology/2015/may/12/how-virtual-world-edge-of-apocalypse-and-back-again (Accessed Feb. 18, 2024).

on strategic alliances, fleet-building and cooperative missions, it is still less of a cold, Social Darwinist vision of a post-human future — one that rewards peaceful cooperation.

No Man's Sky and *Eve Online* both offer the chance to create an avatar that has a meaningful role in the creation of a shared world and story. In Meta's version of these shared spaces, brands lease space temporarily in order to broadcast marketing messages to passive consumers. Mark Zuckerberg will never create a compelling or popular version of a virtual online community without figuring out the sociological alchemy behind *Minecraft* Discord servers. Even if he could, he would only seek to monetize it, missing what qualitative value may otherwise exist in online community.

Like the term "metaverse" itself, Neal Stephenson's cyberpunk classic *Snow Crash*[9] contains the first use of "avatar" to mean a virtual-world proxy for a real-world player. In a much-quoted passage, Stephenson writes: "The people are pieces of software called avatars. They are the audiovisual bodies that people use to communicate with each other in the Metaverse." He later provided some commentary on this definition:

> The words "avatar" (in the sense used here) and "Metaverse" are my inventions, which I came up with when I decided that existing words (such as "virtual reality") were simply too awkward to use.[10]

---

9   Neal Stephenson, *Snow Crash* (Bantam Books, 1992).
10 From Neil Stephenson's introduction to the 2003 Bantam Books reissue of *Snow Crash*, quoted on Wikipedia: https://en.wikiquote.org/wiki/Snow_Crash (Accessed Feb. 18, 2024).

He acknowledges that the term "avatar" and many other aspects of his book's Metaverse appear in a 1986 video game called *Habitat*. Stephenson's version of the concepts in *Snow Crash* was ground-breaking, but the idea of shared virtual worlds, and the prediction that we would inhabit them through proxies, was already a part of humanity's collective consciousness.

Today, the true equivalent of Neal Stephenson's metaverse is closer to the communities built semi-organically around MMORPGs than it is to the dry, antiseptic corporate shell of Zuckerberg's stillborn Metaverse. The question isn't over who will win the race to "build" the first metaverse, but rather who will unite them. Someone will come up with a "killer app" like Tim Berners-Lee's revolutionary invention of the internet browser. Players of each game will cross over into an infinity of virtual worlds, all shared — a sophisticated version of the realities depicted in science fiction stories like *Tron*, *Caprica*, or *Wreck-it-Ralph* (all stories which, perhaps not coincidentally, feature a shadowy corporation or villain seeking to dominate or control the shared space that the characters' avatars inhabit for the sake of profit or power).

Who owns the technology behind that leap forward will define ownership of the spaces created within it. The internet, after all, was initially based on a libertarian premise that the space inside it was infinite. All were welcome to build communities within it, and make their own rules. Hakim Bey anticipated the anarchic multiculturalism of the early internet in the concept of the Temporary Autonomous Zone (or T.A.Z.).[11] The shared universes of gaming culture are already seen as a new market territory, rather

11   Hakim Bey, *T.A.Z.: The Temporary Autonomous Zone* (Autonomedia, 1991).

than a new space for culture and community. Now is the time to ask vital questions about their ownership and independence.

Let's hope the killer app that unites the vast, procedurally-generated universe of a game like *No Man's Sky* with other online worlds is invented by a maverick, an independent, just like Berners-Lee. Otherwise, we are on a trajectory towards another version of the garbage fire internet we inhabit today, only it will be on billboards, and behind our eyes. Fiction writers have already imagined this for us. Novels like *Snow Crash, Neuromancer, Ready Player One* and *The Peripheral* all depict malign corporate or political interests weaponizing or commodifying virtual worlds.

When we imagine the possibilities of the metaverse, we allow ourselves a peek into the infinite. The mathematics of our universe will keep on generating galaxies, stars and planets for what seems like forever — or until it stops. Some kind of metaverse may prove to be where we spend much of our time before that distant end. Its limits will be just as distant, so far out as to be meaningless. We must consider carefully what mathematics and ethics underpin such vast new possible worlds and universes. The technologies that create virtual space are platforms — all just code. The space they create is also very real. We all live in it. Our future could be as full of promise as a sky full of unseen stars, and as dangerous as a planet choked with sentinel drones. With any metaverse either likely to originate as, or become a tool of capitalism, the challenge we face is not to compete over who owns such spaces, but rather to ensure they are peacefully shared, for the benefit of all.

eight

LIMINAL CITY OF
THE SPOTLESS BRAND

> The walls are endlessly bare. Nothing hangs on them,
> nothing defines them. They are without texture. Even
> to the keenest eye or most sentient fingertip, they
> remain unreadable. You will never find a mark there.
> No trace survives. The walls obliterate everything.
> They are permanently absolved of all record. Oblique,
> forever obscure and unwritten. Behold the perfect
> pantheon of absence.[1]
>
> —Mark Z. Danielewski
> *House of Leaves*

T he city center is now a corporate partnership, a place of synergy. This is the capitalist megachurch, the city-as-mall. You
wander down streets thronged with busy foot traffic. A few trees
are segmented into boxed planters, drought-stricken islands land-
locked in a sea of uniform paving stones. The churches and public
squares are treated the same way, frozen amidst blank modernity, like museum pieces locked behind glass. The geography of
the city is fractured and overlaid with walkways that lead only to
window displays, stairs that go nowhere except down into the
yawning, blank mouths of subterranean car parks, herding you
into inhuman spaces with stark angles and nonsensical geography. The polished glass skyscrapers and branded shop fronts are

---

1   Mark Z. Danielewski, *House of Leaves*, (Random House, 2000), p423.

liminal space; between-places. The ever-presence of brands and corporations produces a flatness, an emptiness of human feeling. Much like the endless, featureless hallways in the virally popular video *The Backrooms (Found Footage)*,[2] our cities are now places of blank horror.

Uploaded in January 2022 by the film's young director Kane Pixels, *The Backrooms* explores a mundane labyrinth. Each empty corridor leads to another long, straight corridor or a shadowy alcove, a sheer drop, an impossible staircase. The geography of the space is Escher-like, but there are no curves or bends to trick the eye. In vestibules that resemble underground car parks, footsteps echo behind you as the camera peers from behind pillars and half-shut doors. These interstitial void-spaces are recalled in the antiseptic set design of the 2022 TV show *Severance*, at once a metaphor for the bland, corporate culture of our dismal day jobs and an existential parallel for the bifurcated existence of the show's enslaved "Innies" — the characters' "other selves" who work all night, but remember nothing. This is the nightmare paradox at the heart of the show. For an Innie, work never ends. Both *Severance* and Kane Pixels' *The Backrooms* were directly inspired by an open-source horror (or "creepypasta" — as stated in the previous chapter, a form of copy-paste horror story popularised on Reddit) also known as *The Backrooms*. It emerged from the 4chan image board in 2019, and has inspired a slew of media from indie video games to short fiction and film. Kane Pixels eventually signed a deal to turn his version of the story into a full-scale horror movie with film company A24.

---

2   *The Backrooms (Found Footage)*, directed by Kane Pixels, https://www. youtube.com/watch?v=H4dGpz6cnHo (Accessed Feb. 18, 2024).

In a way, the expansion of the "Backrooms" concept into a fully-fledged mythology slightly devalues the chilling emptiness and half-glimpsed horrors of the original video. A precursor, Sean Wagner's *Marble Hornets*[3] series traded on the aesthetic of abandoned, broken-down, often rural locations. "Backrooms" inspired media explores psychological emptiness and solitude. The liminal spaces between and beneath our world are where the monsters of our subconscious reside, not in the haunted house, or the whispering, witch-haunted woods of Burkittsville in *The Blair Witch Project.*

The Wikipedia page for "The Backrooms" quotes the original 4chan post which started the "creepypasta" meme. It refers to "noclipping" — a phenomenon in video games where the player slips through a wall, ending up in an area of the game which was never meant to be seen or played. The original post reads:

> If you're not careful and you noclip out of reality in the wrong areas, you'll end up in the Backrooms, where it's nothing but the stink of old moist carpet, the madness of mono-yellow, the endless background noise of fluorescent lights at maximum hum-buzz, and approximately six hundred million square miles of randomly segmented empty rooms to be trapped in.[4]

Arriving in the modern city center is like noclipping into the future that corporations and billionaire monopolists want. In many British cities, post-war reconstruction brought brutal slabs of concrete and interlocking ring roads; cities designed for cars,

---

3   *Marble Hornets*, directed by Sean Wagner, https://www.youtube.com/user/marblehornets (Accessed Feb. 18, 2024).

4   Source: https://en.wikipedia.org/wiki/The_Backrooms

not people. More recent regeneration efforts have been more along the lines of private-public partnerships. City centers are divided into "zones" with distinct "characters." This is, of course, substantially powered by corporate investment in the construction of tall glass buildings, whose street-level frontages are leased at discounted rates to giant global and national chains.

In most cities, public space has been annexed. It has undergone a wholesale enclosure into patrolled, corporate-owned "non-places," as defined by French anthropologist Marc Augé.[5] You have no choice but to pass in and out of covered "malls" or "courts" patrolled by yellow-jacketed security guards. Nowhere will you hear the clack and clatter of skateboard wheels or the din of street performers. Our cities have become like airports or American mega-malls, with few places to stop and rest without purchasing a product first.

Of course, the real city is still there if you know where to look. Beneath the pavement, the beach, as the Situationists wrote in the 1960s. Below the corporate substrate, there is culture and community. To the casual observer though, there are only the brands. Want Italian food? There's Vinoteca or Zizzi for the middle classes. Want chicken, or burgers? There's McDonalds and KFC and any other calorific crap you can imagine for the proles. None of these chains sell anything but familiarity. The food, the decor and the vibe are generic and identical, in total synergy with their doppelgangers in a thousand other cities. These are not "places," they are outlets. They offer single-serving "experiences," over once the product is consumed. You are encouraged not to linger in these spaces.

---

5   Marc Augé, *Non-Places: An Introduction to Supermodernity* (Verso Books, 1995).

Despite the wholesale corporate capture of our city centers, there can still be space for art and life. Although as a visitor, this might be difficult or impossible to discern in streets that interlock and overlap; construction-choked alleys that funnel you into enclosed courts. The lustre of the represented corporations corrodes and dissolves as you circle down through Dante-esque levels of a logo-choked hellscape. All this construction, all this expenditure might make a city seem like it is "leveling up"— Boris Johnson's term for giving the poor the opportunity they should rightfully have anyway. Investment is trumpeted as a sign of a city "doing well." In reality, gentrifying an inner city district just forces the poor into the margins, the satellite schemes. Outside the investment zones, things are bleak. No wonder so many of the people who wander the pavements look dazed and lost. Like the protagonist of *The Backrooms* videos, perhaps they are bewildered and overwhelmed by sameness. They search in vain for somewhere to exist that hasn't been colonized by the utterly familiar, somewhere that is not hostile to anyone who has no money to spend. The older, grimier food courts and covered malls will soon be gone, giving way to the brighter, shinier corporate clusters that metastasize between the city's parks and squares, threatening to erupt into profitability. Signs proclaim YOU ARE HERE, and list the brands that will soon appear before you as you aimlessly wander around this particular glass shard. More accurately, they should read YOU ARE NOWHERE. These are places of no place, as Marc Augé writes:

> If a place can be defined as relational, historical, and concerned with identity, then a space which cannot

be defined as relational, historical, and concerned with identity will be a non-place.[6]

To all intents and purposes these city centres are bustling, thriving. They are certainly full of people spending money. But who are they *for*? If the all-corporate centers of our big cities are the alternative to the boarded-up shop fronts and dying high streets of rural and suburban Britain, is that a better solution? The money spent in our cities does not go towards the cities themselves, nor the people that live there, still less the locals who work in these shops for meager wages so they have a few quid to spend in the wide range of Wetherspoons pubs. After the sun goes down, the malls and covered walkways are closed. You have to go around, or underneath, scurry like a rat through subterranean entrances and down narrow, shabby alleyways. You have to navigate the Backrooms to get anywhere; to get nowhere.

Whatever the UK has lost in its long tumble from dubious post-imperial economic and cultural dominance to its current position as a deregulated, bargain-basement America, it still retains traces of weirdness and eccentricity. They are found in areas like Bristol's Gloucester Road and Stokes Croft, which has one of the longest stretches of independent retailers in the UK, and in the dive bars and sweaty clubs of my beloved Glasgow. It's in the quirky villages of the North of England and the Midlands, where locals resist the push to fill up their suburbs with hypermarkets and chain stores while their high streets languish, haunted only by methadone ghosts and the derelict shells of shuttered Costa Coffees. It's in the places that refuse to fail people; but too often these are places where money and wealth are concentrated.

6   Augé, *Non-Places*, p63.

Culture increasingly means privilege. We have failed to recognize this in every town or city where we cede territory to liminal corporate space. We've failed the people who live and work in these cities by giving them nothing real to want, nothing to discover.

The modernized city center has everything you could ever need, of course, as long as you're prepared to buy it from a corporation. They sell every shade of beige and grey. These logos and brands are heralds of the specters that stalk our culture and communities. Despite the bustle, the city center is a wasteland, the scene of a battle fought and lost. You will search long and hard for something that will surprise you, or welcome you as an individual, a human being, and not a consumer. This is the future of our inner cities unless we fight it. The low winter sun colors the anonymous skyscrapers a dull, dusty pink. In the reflective glass, you see only the shadows of the eldritch horrors these nowhere places conceal. The architecture itself is malevolent. Run from it … and don't look back.

nine

PANDORA DYNAMICS

> It is in the very nature of a beginning to carry with
> itself a measure of complete arbitrariness... For a
> moment, the moment of beginning, it is as though the
> beginner had abolished the sequence of temporality
> itself, or as though the actors were thrown out of the
> temporal order and its continuity.[1]
>
> —Hannah Arendt
> *On Revolution*

T o say that a culture has "no future" is not to say that its people cannot survive, just that it must inevitably change in
order for them to endure. The radical unpredictability inherent
in all of the social, cultural, economic, and climatic changes we
now face challenges our old stories. Twentieth-century narratives
often focused on the transmission of our values and histories
beyond our era, the limits of our solar system, or our species.
Now, we seem unwilling or unable to gamble upon the existence
of even our close descendants. Our science fiction is awash with
utopian space opera, high fantasy and aestheticized collapse.
When we predict the future in the stories we tell ourselves, we are
prone to solipsistic, escapist indulgence, even when we imagine
an apocalypse. When we turn to models of statistical or economic
forecasting, we encounter similar biases.

---

1   Hannah Arendt, *On Revolution*, 2016 edn. (Faber and Faber, 1963), p207.

Academic and statistician Peter Turchin's theory of "Clio-dynamics" aims at a less woefully negative forecast of our future than those outlined so far. Synthesizing insights from sociology, history, ethnography, and other disciplines, Turchin's argument is that history itself can become a predictive science. The name is a portmanteau of "Clio," the muse of history in Roman mythology, and "dynamics," which Turchin defines as the study of "temporally varying processes and the search for causal mechanisms."[2] While media coverage of Turchin's theories has often presented them as a form of statistical precognition, he has been quick to lower expectations. He argues that Cliodynamics could be used for social good, perhaps "to encourage the development of social systems in desired directions, and to avoid unintended consequences." Nevertheless, his proclamations about the accuracy and importance of his theory sometimes tend toward the bombastic. Turchin believes: "To truly learn from history, we must transform it into a science."

Isaac Asimov began the sprawling *Foundation*[3] series of stories and novels in 1942 under the shadow of global conflict. In Asimov's tales, the historian Hari Seldon creates a mathematical model much like Turchin's. Feed it the right data, give it a large enough model on which to base its statistical analysis and it can predict the vast sweep of history. Asimov called this model "psychohistory," and gave it a setting as large as our entire galaxy. *Foundation* depicts a human population of billions spread across

---

2   Peter Turchin, "Arise 'Cliodynamics,'" *Nature*, Issue 454, p34–35, https://www.nature.com/articles/454034a

3   Isaac Asimov, *Foundation* (Gnome Press, 1951). The novel was the first published in the series, and combined Asimov's early *Foundation* short stories.

thousands of planets and star systems. Over aeons, Seldon's predictions acquire the charge of prophecy, and inspire religions, revolutions, and wars. They are self-fulfilling, because they are used to guide and predict humanity's course, to steer human culture through dark times. Seldon's legacy, the "foundations" of the series' title, safeguard humanity's history, its data, and its stories. His mathematically-modelled predictions have the same aim as Turchin's Cliodynamics. Seldon and his followers wish to escape the destructive cycles of history by analysing them and turning them into predictive data.

There are other similarities between Turchin's writing and Asimov's schema for the *Foundation* series. Seldon and his disciples begin their story in conflict with an authoritarian empire and its despotic, genetically-cloned rulers. Turchin's theories about where history might go next are also related to the ways in which society produces inequality. He famously predicted in the early 2010s that 2020 would be a year of civil unrest and instability in the United States.[4] Widely rubbished at the time by his fellow academics, his predictions were re-examined in light of the chaos that followed Donald Trump's election loss to Joe Biden in 2020, and the instability and division that the Trump movement whipped up in its wake.

Turchin attributes many of the factors that led to Trump's earlier election to what he calls "elite overproduction." In his analysis of history, an excess of competition for elite roles in society

---

4   Turchin's recent commentary on his 2010 predictions can be read in the paper: "The 2010 Structural-Demographic Forecast for the 2010–2020 Decade: A Retrospective Assessment," *PLoS One*, https://journals.plos.org/plosone/article?id=10.1371/journal.pone.0237458 (Accessed Feb. 18, 2024).

and the inequality this produces and sustains are an accurate bell-wether for that society's collapse. Our swollen middle classes are the threat to society, not revolution from below. Turchin writes that "disgruntled elite-wannabes are far more threatening to societal stability than disgruntled workers."[5] They are the organizers and instigators of insurgent populist movements like Trump's, just as in the past, when middle-class intellectuals formed the vanguard of nineteenth-century revolutionary cabals. While Turchin is always careful not to state outright that correlation implies causation, his predictions point to cycles of history that can be predicted because they have always recurred. Although, like Hari Seldon, Turchin also believes that a sufficiently "scientific" data model might help break that cycle of recurring collapse and chaos, or at least help us understand what must be preserved through the coming of what he calls the "end times" for our current model of liberal democracy, which will be brought about by this dissatisfied elite.

The predictions that arise from Turchin's Cliodynamics can serve as a prescient warning of the consequences of doing nothing. They share this with the messaging of elements within the "climate change" movement — a mixture of catastrophic prognostication, and optimistic promises that crisis can be averted if we pull together, think smarter, try harder. The "effective altruism" movement offers a painfully ironic lesson in the problems of this type of prediction-driven, solution-based thinking. Like Turchin and Seldon, the moral philosopher William MacAskill based his ideas and writing about effective altruism on mathematical

5   Peter Turchin and Mary Harrington, "Will the Elites Ever Behave?" *Unherd*, 10 Jun. 2023, https://unherd.com/2023/06/will-the-elites-ever-behave (Accessed Feb. 18, 2024).

formulae. MacAskill's formula began as a solution to the problems of inequality and privilege. He sought to demonstrate how people with money and power could do the greatest good through their actions and financial donations.

Taken to its logical conclusion, MacAskill's formula dictates that it would make more sense for an elite-educated liberal to take a job in finance and donate a large chunk of their salary to the right charities than it would for the same person to become a doctor, and work saving lives in the developing world. This calculation was based on QALYs — quality-adjusted life years, a way to balance and measure the quality and worth of saved lives. While QALYs might be a useful way to calculate effective spending when considering where to donate money, they became, for many effective altruists, an article of almost religious faith. They could be used to justify the purchase of a mansion for the purpose of hosting events, as one effective altruist foundation backed by MacAskill did in 2021 (according to an interview he gave to Gideon Lewis-Krause of *The New Yorker*[6]). Or QALYs could be used to measure the difference between saving the life of a blind person, versus the life of a paraplegic. MacAskill's mathematics worked just as well for each sum.

If effective altruism offers a cold, deterministic approach to biopolitics, it does so with a polished, utopian, media-friendly sheen. It appeals to politicians, celebrities, activists, corporations, and ordinary people who regularly donate to charity. Despite the very public downfall of multi-billionaire effective altruist Sam

---

6   Gideon Lewis-Krause, "William MacAskill: The Reluctant Prophet of Effective Altruism," *The New Yorker*, Aug. 8, 2022, https://www.newyorker.com/magazine/2022/08/15/the-reluctant-prophet-of-effective-altruism (Accessed Feb. 18, 2024).

Bankman-Fried in one of the biggest cryptocurrency frauds of the 2020s, the movement is alive and well, still the guiding principle behind dozens of charities, nonprofits and NGOs in America, the UK and beyond. MacAskill's QALYs offer a very convenient prediction machine for elite and corporate organisations who wish to appear to be doing good, and to be able to prove it with speculative receipts. The same is true for those who proselytize about it on social media. Effective altruism masquerades as a futures market for moral purity. In practice, as Bankman-Fried's conviction shows, it is just as effective as a mask, for quite the opposite purpose. Lewis-Krause, who published his *New Yorker* piece in 2022 before Bankman-Fried's conviction, said of MacAskill: "He spoke as if… he weren't a person with desires but a tabulating machine through which the profusion of dire global need was assessed, ranked, and processed." In their interview, even MacAskill expressed growing unease with the way his theories have been picked up and applied. Like all prophets, he seems to have reached a point where he realizes that his predictions are also a burden — that the apparent gift of foresight is also a curse.

The philosopher Amia Srinivasan knew MacAskill at Cambridge. She watched the rise of the effective altruism movement up close. Now a Professor of Social and Political Theory at Oxford, in 2015 she wrote a searing critique of the morality of approaching such questions with mathematical precision. "Effective altruism doesn't try to understand how power works, except to better align itself with it," she argued in her review of MacAskill's first book.[7] "In this sense, it leaves everything just as it is…

---

7   Amia Srinivasan, "Stop the Robot Apocalypse," *London Review of Books*, Sep. 24, 2015, https://www.lrb.co.uk/the-paper/v37/n18/amia-srinivasan/stop-the-robot-apocalypse (Accessed Feb. 18, 2024).

QALYs free us from the specificity of people's lives, giving us a universal currency for misery." Srinivasan highlights the human cost of calculating and donating rather than acting and doing, in the company of others. She highlights the ways in which these real-world, communal actions matter, but are missed by MacAskill's calculus:

> What's the expected marginal value of becoming an anti-capitalist revolutionary? To answer that you'd need to put a value and probability measure on achieving an unrecognisably different world — even, perhaps, on our becoming unrecognisably different sorts of people. It's hard enough to quantify the value of a philanthropic intervention: how would we go about quantifying the consequences of radically reorganising society?

For Srinivasan, the focus on solving "downstream" problems like the prospect of rogue artificial intelligence was the logical conclusion of weighing one life against another in order to predict who to save. In the grand scale, what are the lives of everyone currently alive truly worth, if weighed against the lives of our future descendants? Save one person now, or save a million in a hundred years? Srinivasan thought the basic principle of donating to do the most good was sound. With its evolution into what MacAskill, Nick Bostrom, and other effective altruist thinkers called "longtermism," the movement became little more than speculative fiction. All predictive systems face this crisis. If they attempt to tell the truth about the future, like Turchin and Seldon, they are doomed to not be believed until history proves them right. If they use their predictions to *shape* the future, then like MacAskill's movement, they become an open church for fraudulent hucksters like Bankman-Fried. This happens because of, not despite, the religious zeal of its converts. Read interviews with Sam Bankman-Fried before his conviction and you get the sense of a big-tent revivalist who has just healed his own broken shins. He believed his own narrative, and in the end he went down swinging in court, still arguing to justify his eight billion dollar fraud as a worthwhile activity in effective altruist terms.

Most of us are not mathematicians, so these predictive formulae are comprehensible to us in the same way as a magic spell, or the operating system of a mobile phone. We do not need to understand. If someone we find credible tells us they work, we believe them. It's impossible for the average person to say whether Turchin's analysis or MacAskill's calculus succeed on a mathematical level. Even if Turchin's model is correct, is it useful if all it has to offer us is apocalypse, or the maintenance of the present state of affairs? If MacAskill's mathematics work, but they are put into service by a group of interests who would be perfectly happy to watch much of humanity go extinct as long as the majority with "quality of life" survive, what are they worth? These narratives are not so different to the stakes seen in our naffest "young adult fantasy" dystopias, such as *The Hunger Games* or the *Divergent* series. Perhaps utopian, half-joke concepts such as technologically-driven post-scarcity of the *Star Trek* variety, or home-grown left-wing variants in the vein of Aaron Bastani's *Fully Automated Luxury Communism*[8] are still preferable territories for our imaginary and imagined futures. At least they hold out hope of definitively solving the problems of instability, inequality, and injustice. These are

---

8   Aaron Bastani, *Fully-Automated Luxury Communism* (Verso Books, 2019).

nice dreams. The "scientific" solutions and analyses presented by MacAskill or Turchin offer much the same thing — both could be accused of achieving the opposite; merely offering a vector through which capital can maintain the status quo by "influencing" the right social and economic trends. They offer the illusion of control in the face of the very real prospect of collapse.

The other function of Hari Seldon's Foundation was to serve as an "ark" containing the history, art and storytelling of the people of the empire, so that their culture would survive its inevitable fall. The writer and futurist Joshua Ellis once asked me why, within all our fictional futures, nobody has kept hold of a Haynes manual.[9] This is a relevant question for anyone who fears the kind of collapse Turchin predicts in the next decade. How do we preserve that which might prove useful? Perhaps this is the only question with any merit. A post-collapse society is likely to be similar in many ways to the present world, in that it will be uneven. Infrastructure will be patchy, in places it will disappear. Those who know how to fix things, who have preserved the knowledge and skills of the culture that is collapsing around them, will hold social capital.

The goal of Seldon's Foundation is to preserve knowledge and skills for a new beginning, long beyond the darkest days of collapse. This is a similar proposition to the one the retired English teacher Professor Faber makes to the "fireman" Guy Montag in *Fahrenheit 451*. The plot of Ray Bradbury's 1953 novel revolves

---

9   Haynes Owner's Workshop Manuals are a series of manuals from the British publisher Haynes Publishing Group. The series focuses primarily on the maintenance and repair of automotive vehicles. Joshua Ellis and I discuss this in episode 20 of the podcast Strange Exiles (Oct. 6, 2023), Spotify, https://open.spotify.com/episode/2cGSs1MWNPmTSMUfd-jSE91 (Accessed Feb. 18, 2024).

around a community who memorize great works of literature to prevent them being burned by a totalitarian regime. Faber tells Montag: "Don't ask for guarantees. And don't look to be saved in any one thing, person, machine, or library. Do your own bit of saving, and if you drown, at least die knowing you were heading for shore."[10] This concept of "saving" is not what Turchin recommends; he stops short of offering Cliodynamics as a predictive science to be used to avoid catastrophe. MacAskill's QALYs place little or no value on artworks or literature. In contrast, Seldon's psychohistory does not presume to save "us," but rather culture — the "stuff" which makes us. These are all tragic propositions, because they presume the inevitable loss of the present. If the present is irredeemably broken, how long can we defer tragedy?

The theme of the preservation of knowledge after the fall is echoed in Russell Hoban's 1980 post-apocalyptic masterpiece *Riddley Walker*.[11] Very little survives the collapse, and the aftermath that Hoban's novel describes. His beleaguered protagonists live in crushing destitution in a barren, poisoned landscape. Even the English language has degraded and devolved into guttural, monosyllabic slang. The only culture or literature left is a traveling Punch and Judy show that tours the muddy, neo-medieval villages left in the wake of some unnameable, world-destroying event. In the course of the novel the protagonist regains the secret of nuclear fission, the same secret that destroyed the world. He is deaf to its meaning, unable to understand the knowledge he encounters; only aware of its grim significance. In Hoban's bleak conclusion, knowledge is useless. Even if it is preserved, it nonetheless loses its power.

---

10 Ray Bradbury, *Fahrenheit 451*, 2013 edn. (Simon & Schuster, 1953), p82.
11 Russell Hoban, *Riddley Walker* (Jonathan Cape, 1980).

At various points in human history, people have sought to preserve their knowledge and culture in the face of persecution, war, or outright extinction. In early 17th century Amsterdam, the practice of Protestant "tolerance" allowed a tight-knit community of Jewish refugees to thrive within the city, despite laws that still forbade their public worship and assembly.[12] The city became home to two synagogues, mostly attended by Shepardi Jews who had settled there after leaving North Africa and Portugal, either seeking mercantile opportunities, or fleeing persecution — sometimes both. These communities produced noted intellectuals, scholars, publishers and thinkers, including Menasseh Ben Israel, an early teacher of the philosopher Baruch Spinoza. Among other topics of religious scholarship, Ben Israel was interested in kabbalah, the Jewish mystic tradition. He would go on to found the first of several printing presses in the city,[13] disseminating kabbalistic knowledge alongside more traditional Jewish religious texts. Historians Eliezer Baumgarten and Uri Safrai write:

> Jewish life and literary productions in seventeenth-century Amsterdam were marked by the multiple crossroads of that early modern Dutch metropolis; finance, trade, diplomacy, but also the cross-cultural and interconfessional encounters of the printing shop and the city at large... [Amsterdam] served as

---

12 Steven Nadler, "Rembrandt's Jews," University of Chicago Press, https://press.uchicago.edu/Misc/Chicago/567362.html (Accessed Feb. 18, 2024).

13 Steven Nadler, "The Amsterdam Rabbi who Became the Most Famous Jew in the World," Zocalo, 5 Sep. 2018, https://www.zocalopublicsquare.org/2018/09/05/amsterdam-rabbi-became-famous-jew-world/ideas/essay (Accessed Feb. 18, 2024).

an important crossroads for diverse Kabbalistic and
magical traditions... nearly every rabbinic leader in
Amsterdam had some connection to these traditions.[14]

Many of the Jewish people seeking refuge in 17th-century
Holland were simply looking for a better life. For Menasseh Ben
Israel, living there was also about preserving, sharing and spread-
ing the knowledge of the Jewish people through yet another
century of pogroms and expulsions. That he managed to preserve,
re-print and distribute this knowledge — including the traditions
of kabbalah — despite the climate of fear and discrimination
against all Jewish people is nothing short of a miracle. He not only
influenced subsequent scholars of both kabbalah and the Torah,
he also ensured that the thoughts of mystics and teachers from
centuries long past would endure. Many of the texts he printed
are preserved today in one of Amsterdam's most curious muse-
ums, the Embassy of the Free Mind,[15] alongside a huge library of
esoteric books and tracts on subjects such as theosophy, spiritual-
ism and demonology. Whether these magickal systems proved to
be true, falsifiable or even useful is rarely debated these days. We
have for the most part moved on from traditions like kabbalah,
just as we have stopped believing in the spirit world or demonic

---

14 Eliezer Baumgarten and Uri Safrai, "Rabbi Moshe Zacuto and the Kab-
    balistic Circle of Amsterdam," Amsterdam University Press, 1 Nov. 2020,
    https://www.aup-online.com/content/journals/10.5117/SR2020.1-
    2.002.BAUM?crawler=true (Accessed Feb. 18, 2024).

15 A short essay about the contents and history of the Embassy of the Free
    Mind and its origins in 17th century Amsterdam's publishing industry can
    be read at: https://embassyofthefreemind.com/nl/embassy-of-the-free-
    mind-nl/over-de-embassy-of-the-free-mind-nl/amsterdam-als-vrijhaven
    (Accessed Feb. 18, 2024).

possession outside of the cheap jump-scares of Hollywood horror movies. Kabbalah, like Cliodynamics, QALYs and psychohistory, is a way of using mathematics to interpret the world. Like kabbalah, these theories are interesting. They have merit as a way of understanding ourselves, our history, and our possible futures. But in all probability, like kabbalah, the books that contain them will end up on dusty shelves, mostly forgotten. Hopefully there will be an embassy there to house them.

Perhaps we can group all of these predictive mathematical systems under the umbrella label of "Cassandradynamics" — the theories and prognostications of prophets destined not to be believed, and yet to be proved true. In most versions of the Greek myth, Cassandra meets a sticky end. Her predictions of the fall of Troy doom her in the anticipation of catastrophe, and make her despised in its wake. There's no joy of prophecy in Cassandra's story. Rather, like MacAskill, she is often portrayed as a character at the mercy of the whims of cruel fate, her predictions manipulated and co-opted by the powerful, and thus robbed of their potential to protect or divert the course of history. Turchin seems likely to share this fate, too. Either collapse will happen, and we will all look back and say he was right. Or we will avoid it, despite his help, and he will be proved wrong. For MacAskill, the worst has already happened — the elites he sought to reform swallowed him whole, and spat him back out. He and his disciples will never live long enough to know if their money was well-spent. Hari Seldon's story is at least instructive. Psychohistory is questioned, interrogated, and shown wanting in Asimov's saga, although it takes aeons for the results to be tabulated. And yet, it succeeds — because human culture endures.

Perhaps instead of these Cassandradynamic systems, we could seek to follow one based on Pandoradynamics. In the story of Pandora's box, all of the evils of the world are contained within a locked chest. When it is opened, war, famine, and greed are released into the world to torment mankind. At the bottom of the now almost empty chest, one thing remains. In most tellings, this is described as "hope." Philosophers have argued over the meaning of this for centuries. Is hope the last item because despite all the evils of the world, good will triumph? Or is hope the last item because it is the most painful burden to bear in a world whose dark fate is already sealed? It is perhaps best to leave this question unresolved. The only thing worse than having false hope is knowing that hope is false. Antonio Gramsci's oft-quoted maxim is that we must maintain "pessimism of the intellect, optimism of the will." A Pandoradynamic variation of this formula might read, "pessimism of the prediction, mystery of our hopes."

And what to hope for, in a world where we have almost everything, but stand to lose it? Hannah Arendt thought long and hard about this in her treatise *On Revolution*, which explores the ideas and events that led to the French and American revolutions. In the latter chapters, she writes about how both revolutions took inspiration from the republican ideals of ancient Rome, and the concept of "foundation." For Arendt, this moment of foundation is one of "beginning again" — of claiming freedom, and establishing a *novus ordo seclorum* (new world order). If this can be done in the name of freedom, Arendt argues that it is worth hoping for, and fighting for. She argues that freedom comes *after* inequality and suffering are solved, and not before. She writes of the false promise of the "American dream":

> While it is true that freedom can come only to those whose needs have been fulfilled, it is equally true that it will escape those who are bent upon living for their desires. The American dream [...] was unhappily, the dream of a promised land where milk and honey flow. And the fact that the development of modern technology was so soon able to realize this dream beyond anyone's wildest expectation quite naturally had the effect of confirming for the dreamers that they had really come to live in the best of all possible worlds.[16]

As she foresaw, the promise that technology would deliver an unbroken path to progress and prosperity was bound to be undermined by historical events. She saw that all revolutions could lead to tyranny, but that none could lead to utopia — rather, the more the leaders and thinkers of a movement tried to predict history, the more likely they were to become tyrants who enforced the reality of their predictions, and the more likely their revolutions were to become dictatorships and not democracies. For Arendt, the moment of foundation, of beginning, was more important than the revolutionary moment. The constitution of a new order was only as strong as the promises the revolutionaries made to one another, and how accountable they would remain to those compacts. Arendt writes that "there is an element of the world-building capacity of man in the human faculty of making and keeping promises."[17]

This is how we build, this is how we begin. A story told and a promise made. Like Pandora, we find hope at the bottom

---

16 Hannah Arendt, *On Revolution*, 2016 edn. (Faber and Faber, 1963), p137.

17 Arendt, *On Revolution*, p174-175.

of despair. No intelligence, no mathematics, no history, and no theory can divine for us whether that hope is real, or a cruel illusion. We must resist such totalizing systems, which destroy as they create. Instead we must preserve. We are archivists and record-keepers. We are storytellers and liars, and we lie to ourselves most often. Perhaps when our distant descendants visit or unearth the libraries that remain, they will be unable to discern lies from stories, science from magic, or records from dusty propaganda. Our descendants could be few, or they could be many. Will they understand what they read? Perhaps not. They may yet find it beautiful, even useful.

BIBLIOGRAPHY

Anthony, Dave and Corky, Lehmkuhl, directors. *Call of Duty, Black Ops*. Treyarch and Activision. Sony PlayStation 3. 2010.

Antosca, Nick, creator. *Channel Zero*. SyFy, 2016 - 2018.

Arendt, Hannah. *On Revolution*. London: Faber and Faber, 1963.

———. *On Violence*. New York: Houghton Mifflin Harcourt, 1970.

Asimov, Isaac. *Foundation*. New York: Gnome Press, 1951.

Aubuchon, Remi and Moore, Ronald D., creators. *Caprica*. Syfy, 2010.

Augé, Marc. *Non-Places: An Introduction to Supermodernity*. 5th ed. London: Verso Books, 2008.

Avakian, Bob. "A New Year, The Urgent Need For A Radically New World — For The Emancipation Of All Humanity." Revcom.us, Jan. 1 2021, https://revcom.us/en/avakian/new-years-statement-2021/bob-avakian-new-years-statement-2021-en.html

Banks, Iain M. *Consider Phlebas*. London: Macmillan, 1987.

Barnes, John. *Kaleidoscope Century*. New York: Tor Books, 1995.

Basciano, Oliver. "When We Grew up, Luis Bunuel was on Channel 4: The Proudly Highbrow Otolith Group." *The Guardian*, Jul. 6, 2022, https://www.theguardian.com/artanddesign/2022/jul/06/luis-bunuel-channel-4-proudly-highbrow-otolith-group-apocalypse

Bastani, Aaron. *Fully-Automated Luxury Communism*. London: Verso Books, 2019.

Baszucki, David, director. *Roblox*. Roblox Corporation. Microsoft Windows. 2006.

Baumgarten, Eliezer and Safrai, Uri. "Rabbi Moshe Zacuto and the Kabbalistic Circle of Amsterdam", Amsterdam University Press, Nov. 1 2020, https://www.aup-online.com/content/journals/10.5117/SR2020.1-2.002.BAUM?crawler=true

Bey, Hakim. *T.A.Z.: The Temporary Autonomous Zone*. New York: Autonomedia, 1991.

Blackmore, Susan. *The Meme Machine*. Oxford: Oxford University Press, 1999.

Bond, Neil L. "How EVE Online's Players Started a War That's Cost $700K." IGN, https://www.ign.com/articles/how-eve-onlines-players-started-a-war-thats-cost-700k

Bostrom, Nick. "Genetic Enhancement and the Future of Humanity." *The European Magazine*, 2011, archived at https://web.archive.org/web/20181231163914/https://www.theeuropean-magazine.com/nick-bostrom--2/6028-genetic-enhancement-and-the-future-of-humanity

———. "The Simulation Argument." *Philosophical Quarterly*, 2003, Vol. 53, No. 211.

———. "The Vulnerable World hypothesis." *Global Policy*, Vol. 10, Issue 4, 2019, https://nickbostrom.com/papers/vulnerable.pdf

Braben, David and Bell, Ian. *Elite*. Acornsoft. BBC Micro. 1984.

Bradbury, Ray. *Fahrenheit 451*. New York: Simon & Schuster, 1953.

Brooker, Charlie. "In Conversation with Adam Curtis." *Vice*, Feb. 11, 2021, https://www.vice.com/en/article/4ad8db/adam-curtis-charlie-brooker-cant-get-you-out-of-my-head

Brown, Alex. "Here's how NASA thinks society will collapse." *The Atlantic*, Mar. 18, 2014, https://www.theatlantic.com/politics/archive/2014/03/heres-how-nasa-thinks-society-will-collapse/441375

Burger, Neil, director. *Divergent*. Lionsgate, 2014.

Byrne, Rhonda. *The Secret*. New York: Atria Books / Beyond Worlds Publishing, 2006.

Cadwalladr, Carole. "The Great British Brexit Robbery." *The Guardian*, May 7, 2017, https://www.theguardian.com/technology/2017/may/07/the-great-british-brexit-robbery-hijacked-democracy

Caffo, Leonardo. "A Conversation with Slavoj Žižek." *Public Seminar*, Oct. 20, 2021, https://publicseminar.org/essays/a-conversation-with-slavoj-zizek

Cameron, James, director. *The Terminator*. Orion Pictures, 1984.

Campbell, Joseph. *The Hero with A Thousand Faces*. New York: Pantheon Books, 1949.

Churchwell, Sarah. "Can American Democracy Survive Donald Trump?" *The Guardian*, Nov. 21, 2020, https://www.theguardian.com/books/2020/nov/21/can-american-democracy-survive-donald-trump

Cliffe, Jerry. "The Rise of the Bio-surveillance State." *New Statesman*, Mar. 25, 2020, https://www.newstatesman.com/long-reads/2020/03/rise-bio-surveillance-state

Cline, Ernest. *Ready Player One*. New York: Crown Publishing Group, 2011.

Cole, Yussef, "The Hollow Nihilism of Call of Duty", *Wired*, 2020, https://www.wired.com/story/call-of-duty-black-ops-history

Cuarón, Alfonso, director. *Children of Men*. Universal Pictures, 2006.

Danielewski, Mark Z. *House of Leaves*. New York: Random House, 2000.

Darabont, Frank, developer. *The Walking Dead*. AMC Studios, 2010-2022.

Davies, William. *Nervous States*. New York: W.W. Norton & Co., 2018.

Deb, Siddartha. "Stranger Than Fiction." *The Baffler*, Jun. 5, 2017, https://thebaffler.com/contraband/stranger-than-fiction

Deleuze, Gilles and Guattari, Felix. "Postscript on the Societies of Control." October, Vol. 59, 1992, https://www.jstor.org/stable/778828

DiBiase, Antonella. "What is Neurocapitalism and Why Are We Living In It?'" *Vice Magazine*, Oct. 16, 2016, https://www.vice.com/en/article/qkjxaq/what-is-neurocapitalism-and-why-are-we-living-in-it

Dick, Philip K. (ed. Pamela Jackson and Jonathan Lethem). *The Exegesis of Phillip K. Dick*. New York: Houghton Mifflin Harcourt, 2011.

———. *Valis*. New York: Bantam Books, 1981.

Doctorow, Cory. "Theresa May Wants to Ban Crypto." *Boing Boing*, Jun. 4, 2017, https://boingboing.net/2017/06/04/theresa-may-king-canute.html

Drexler, K. Eric. *Engines of Creation: The Coming Era of Nanotechnology*. New York: Doubleday, 1986.

Dvorsky, George. "New Report on Emerging AI Risks Paints a Grim Future." *Gizmodo*, Feb. 21, 2018, https://gizmodo.com/new-report-on-ai-risks-paints-a-grim-future-1823191087

Eaton, George. "Andreas Malm: 'The Likely Future is Escalating Catastrophe.'" *New Statesman*, Oct. 14, 2020, https://www.newstatesman.com/encounter/2020/10/andreas-malm-likely-future-escalating-catastrophe

Erickson, Dan, creator. *Severance*. Apple TV+, 2022 - present.

European Court of Auditors. "Combating Desertification in the EU." Publications Office of the European Union, 2018, https://op.europa.eu/webpub/eca/special-reports/desertification-33-2018/en/

Fatum Project. "Theory: The Fatum Project." Randonautica, https://www.randonautica.com/theory

Fisher, Mark. *Capitalist Realism: Is There No Alternative?* London: Zer0 Books, 2009.

Ford, Fred and Reiche, Paul III, designers. *Star Control II: The Ur-Quan Masters*. Accolade and Crystal Dynamics. MS-DOS. 1992.

Foucault, Michel. *Discipline and Punish*. New York: Pantheon Books, 1977.

Fukasaku, Kinji, director. *Battle Royale*, Toei Company, 2000.

German, Aleksei, director. *Hard to Be a God*. Netflix, 2013.

Gibson, William. *Neuromancer*. New York: Ace, 1984.

———. *Pattern Recognition*. New York: GP Putnam's & Sons, 2003.

———. *The Peripheral*. New York: GP Putnam's & Sons, 2014.

Giroux, Henry A. "Depoliticisation is a Deadly Weapon of Neoliberal Fascism." *Truthout*, Oct. 15, 2019, https://truthout.org/articles/depoliticization-is-a-deadly-weapon-of-neoliberal-fascism

Gray, James, director. *Ad Astra*. 20th Century Fox, 2019.

Gray, John. "Dear Google, Please Solve Death." *New Statesman*, Apr. 9, 2017, https://www.newstatesman.com/culture/2017/04/dear-google-please-solve-death

———. "The Myth of Natural Morality." *New Statesman*, Nov. 25, 2020, https://www.newstatesman.com/ideas/2020/11/whats-wrong-with-rights-nigel-biggar-review

———. *Straw Dogs: Thoughts on Humans and Other Animals*. London: Granta, 2003.

———. "What Sun Tzu Knew." *New Statesman*, Jan. 29, 2020, https://www.newstatesman.com/long-reads/2020/01/sun-tzu-the-art-war-politics

Guerrero, Jean. "My Father Says He's a 'Targeted Individual.' Maybe We All Are." *Wired*, Oct. 25, 2018, https://www.wired.com/story/my-father-says-hes-a-targeted-individual-maybe-we-all-are

Haidt, Jonathan. "Why the Past Ten Years of American Life Have Been Uniquely Stupid." *The Atlantic*, Apr. 11, 2022, https://www.theatlantic.com/magazine/archive/2022/05/social-media-democracy-trust-babel/629369

Haldeman, Joe. *The Forever War*. New York: St Martin's Press, 1974.

Hall, Stuart (ed. Davison, Sally, Featherstone, David, Rustin, Michael and Schwarz, Bill). *Selected Political Writings*. Durham: Duke University Press, 2017.

Han, Byung-Chul. "I Practise Philosophy as Art." *ArtReview*, Dec. 2, 2021, https://artreview.com/byung-chul-han-i-practise-philosophy-as-art

———. *Psychopolitics: Neoliberalism and New Technologies of Power*. London: Verso Books, 2014.

Harmon, Dan, creator. *Community*. NBC, 2009-2014.

——— and Roiland, Justin, creators. *Rick and Morty*. Netflix, 2013-present day, https://www.netflix.com/title/80014749

Herbert, Frank. *Dune*. Boston: Chilton Books, 1965.

Hickel, Jason and Kirk, Martin. "Are You Ready to Consider That Capitalism is the Real Problem?" *Fast Company*, Nov. 7, 2017, https://www.fastcompany.com/40439316/are-you-ready-to-consider-that-capitalism-is-the-real-problem

Hickel, Jason. "To Deal With Climate Change We Need a New Financial System." *The Guardian*, Nov. 5, 2016, https://www.theguardian.com/global-development-professionals-network/2016/nov/05/how-a-new-money-system-could-help-stop-climate-change

Hoban, Russell. *Riddley Walker*. London: Jonathan Cape, 1980.

Hofstadter, Richard. "The Paranoid Style in American Politics." *Harpers*, 1964, https://harpers.org/archive/1964/11/the-paranoid-style-in-american-politics

Hyams, Peter, director. *2010: The Year We Make Contact*. Metro Goldwyn Mayer, 1984.

Jackson, Mick, director. *Threads*. BBC and Nine Network Australia, 1984.

James, P.D. *The Children of Men*. London: Faber and Faber, 1992.

Klein, Naomi. "How Big Tech Plans to Profit from the Pandemic." *The Guardian*, May 13, 2020, https://www.theguardian.com/news/2020/oct/15/dangerous-rise-of-military-ai-drone-swarm-autonomous-weapons

Kruse, Michael. "Roger Stone's Last Dirty Trick." *Politico*, Jan. 25, 2019, https://www.politico.com/magazine/story/2019/01/25/roger-stone-last-dirty-trick-224217

Kubrick, Stanley, director. *2001: A Space Odyssey*. Metro Goldwyn Mayer, 1968.

Lengfelder, Joshua and Salcedo, Auburn, creators. *Randonatica*. Fatum Project. iOs. 2020.

Lewis-Krause, Gideon. "William MacAskill: The Reluctant Prophet of Effective Altruism." *The New Yorker*, Aug. 8, 2022, https://www.newyorker.com/magazine/2022/08/15/the-reluctant-prophet-of-effective-altruism

Ligotti, Thomas. *The Conspiracy Against The Human Race*. New York: Hippocampus Press, 2010.

Lisberger, Steven, director. *Tron*. Walt Disney Productions, 1982.

Lucas, George, director. *Star Wars*. Twentieth Century Fox, 1977.

Miller, George, director. *Mad Max*. Warner Brothers, 1979.

———. *Mad Max 2: Beyond Thunderdome*. Warner Brothers, 1985.

———. *Mad Max: Fury Road*. Warner Brothers, 2015.

Moore, Alan, Gibbons, Dave, and Higgins, John. *Watchmen*. New York: DC Comics, 1986-1987.

Moore, Rich, director. *Wreck-It Ralph*. Walt Disney Pictures, 2012

Morgan, Richard K. *Altered Carbon*. London: Victor Gollancz, 2002.

Morningstar, Chip, director. *Habitat*. Lucasfilm Games, Quantum Link and Fujitsu. Commodore 64. 1986.

Moss, Jeremiah. "Open House: Welcome to New York, Now Go Home." *N Plus One*, 2020, https://www.nplusonemag.com/issue-36/essays/open-house

Murakami, Haruki. *Hard-Boiled Wonderland and The End of the World*. Tokyo: Kodansha International, 1985.

Murray, Sean, creator. *No Man's Sky*. Hello Games. Sony PlayStation 4. 2016.

Myrick, Daniel and Sánchez, Eduardo, directors. *The Blair Witch Project*. Artisan Entertainment, 1999.

Nadler, Steven. "The Amsterdam Rabbi who Became the Most Famous Jew in the World." Zocalo, 5 Sep. 2018, https://www.zocalopublicsquare.org/2018/09/05/amsterdam-rabbi-became-famous-jew-world/ideas/essay

———. "Rembrandt's Jews." University of Chicago Press, https://press.uchicago.edu/Misc/Chicago/567362.html

Nenquimo, Nemonte. "This is My Message to the Western World - Your Civilisation is Killing Life on Earth." *The Guardian*, Oct. 12, 2020, https://www.theguardian.com/commentisfree/2020/oct/12/western-worldyour-civilisation-killing-life-on-earth-indigenous-amazon-planet

Niggli, Laura, Huggel, Christian, Muccione, Veruska, Neukom, Raphael and Salzmann, Nadine. "Towards Improved Understanding of Cascading and Interconnected Risks from Concurrent Weather Extremes." *PLoS*, Aug. 10, 2022, https://journals.plos.org/climate/article?id=10.1371/journal.pclm.0000057

Nolan, Christopher, director. *Interstellar*. Paramount Pictures and Warner Brothers, 2014.

Nomura, Tatsuo, director. *Pokémon GO*. Niantic. iOs. 2016.

Nordgren, Andie, producer. *Eve Online*. CCP Games. Microsoft Windows. 2003.

Park, Taejin, Hashimoto, Hirofumi, Wang, Weile, Thrasher, Bridget, Michaelis, Andrew R., Lee, Tsengdar, Brosnan, Ian G. and Nemani, Ramakrishna R. "What Does Global Land Climate Look Like at 2°C Warming?" Dec. 20, 2022, *Advanced Earth and Space Sciences*, https://agupubs.onlinelibrary.wiley.com/doi/10.1029/2022EF003330

Parker, Trey, director. *South Park* (Seres 11, Episode 10). South Park Studios, 2007.

Parkin, Simon. "Eve Online: How a Virtual World Went to the Edge of Apocalypse and Back." *The Guardian*, May 12, 2015, https://www.theguardian.com/technology/2015/may/12/how-virtual-world-edge-of-apocalypse-and-back-again

Pasquale, Frank. "Machines Set Loose to Slaughter." *The Guardian*, Oct. 15, 2020, https://www.theguardian.com/news/2020/oct/15/dangerous-rise-of-military-ai-drone-swarm-autonomous-weapons

Penny, Laurie. "This Is Not the Apocalypse You Were Looking For." *Wired*, Mar. 30, 2020, https://www.wired.com/story/coronavirus-apocalypse-myths

Persson, Markus and Bergensten, Jens, designers. *Minecraft*. Mojang Studios. macOS. 2011.

Pixels, Kane, director. *The Backrooms (Found Footage)*. YouTube, Jan. 7, 2022, https://www.youtube.com/watch?v=H4dGpz6cnHo

Pletcher, Adam, designer. *Descent: FreeSpace - The Great War*. Interplay Productions. Microsoft Windows. 1998.

Ramis, Harold, director. *Groundhog Day*. Columbia Pictures, 1993.

Rees, Martin. "NASA's Webb Telescope is a Joy. But it's the Private Ventures That Push at its Limits." *The Guardian*, Jan. 2, 2022, https://www.theguardian.com/commentisfree/2022/jan/02/james-webb-space-telescope-thrilling-future-for-mankind

Reider, Travis. "Why We Should Have Fewer Children to Save the Planet." *The Guardian*, Sep. 12, 2016, https://www.theguardian.com/commentisfree/2016/sep/12/why-we-should-have-fewer-children-save-the-planet-climate-change

Rivera, Alex, director. *Sleep Dealer*. Maya Entertainment, 2008.

Roddenberry, Gene, creator. *Star Trek: The Original Series*. Desilu Productions, Paramount Television, and the Norway Corporation, 1966-1969.

Ross, Gary, director. *The Hunger Games*. Lionsgate, 2012.

Rushkoff, Douglas. "Survival of the Richest." OneZero, Jul. 5, 2018, https://onezero.medium.com/survival-of-the-richest-9ef-6cddd0cc1

Russo, Anthony and Russo, Joe, directors. *Avengers: Endgame*. Marvel Studios and Walt Disney Studios, 2019.

Scott, Ridley, director. *Alien*. 20th Century Fox and Brandywine Productions, 1979.

———— . *The Martian*. 20th Century Studios, 2015.

Srinivasan, Amia. "Stop the Robot Apocalypse." *London Review of Books*, Sep. 24, 2015, https://www.lrb.co.uk/the-paper/v37/n18/amia-srinivasan/stop-the-robot-apocalypse

Stapleton, Olaf. *Star Maker*. London: Methuen, 1937.

Steffen, Alex. "The Outquisition." Medium, Jun. 16, 2016, https://medium.com/@AlexSteffen/the-outquisition-3e15cb889032

Stephenson, Neal. *Snow Crash*. New York: Bantam Books, 1992.

———— . Introduction to *Snow Crash*, 2003 edn. New York: Bantam Books, 1992. Quoted in: Wikipedia, https://en.wikiquote.org/wiki/Snow_Crash

Stokel-Walker, Chris. "The complicated truth about TikTok and Tourette's syndrome." *Vice*, Mar. 27, 2021, https://www.wired.co.uk/article/tiktok-tourettes

Stone, Roger. *Stone's Rules: How to Win at Politics, Business, and Style*. New York: Skyshore Publishing, 2018.

Straczynski, J. Michael, creator. *Babylon 5*. Warner Brothers Television, 1993–1998.

People Can Fly and Epic Games, developers. *Fortnite: Battle Royale*. Epic Games. Sony PlayStation 4. 2017.

Taete, Jamie-Lee. "I Followed the 'Randonaut' App Wherever It Wanted to Take Me." *Vice*, Jul. 17, 2020, https://www.vice.com/en/article/bv8dk4/jamie-lee-curtis-taete-randonaut-photos

Takami, Koushun (trans. Oniki, Yuji). *Battle Royale*. San Francisco: Viz Media, 2003.

Turchin, Peter. "Arise 'Cliodynamics.'" *Nature*, Issue 454, Jul. 2, 2008, https://www.nature.com/articles/454034a

——— . "The 2010 Structural-Demographic Forecast for the 2010–2020 Decade: A Retrospective Assessment", *PLoS One*, https://journals.plos.org/plosone/article?id=10.1371/journal.pone.0237458

——— and Harrington, Mary, "Will the Elites Ever Behave?", *Unherd*, June 10, 2023, https://unherd.com/2023/06/will-the-elites-ever-behave

Turner, Ken, director. *Call of Duty*. Infinity Ward Inc. and Activision. Sony PlayStation 3. 2003.

Villeneuve, Denis, director. *Arrival*. Paramount Pictures, 2016.

———. *Blade Runner 2049*. Warner Brothers, 2017.

———. *Dune: Part One*. Warner Brothers, 2021.

Wachowski, Lana and Wachowski, Lily, directors. *The Matrix*. Warner Brothers, 1999.

Wagner, Sean, director. *Marble Hornets* (multiple videos). YouTube, Jun. 20, 2009 - present. https://www.youtube.com/user/marblehornets

Watson, Mike. *Can the Left Learn to Meme?* London: Zer0 Books, 2018.

——— . *The Memeing of Mark Fisher*. London: Zer0 Books, 2021.

Wise, Robert, director. *Star Trek: The Motion Picture*. Paramount Pictures, 1979.

Žižek, Slavoj. "For a Left That Dares To Speak Its Name." Institute for the Radical Imagination, Oct. 8, 2019, https://youtu.be/qxz4zkO_ce4

———. *Living in the End Times*. London: Verso Books, 2010.

———. *Pandemic! Covid 19 shakes the world*. Cambridge: Polity, 2020.

ACKNOWLEDGEMENTS

Many people helped to shape these essays whether they knew it or not. Most of all my wife Amber, the most patient, loyal and honest partner I could hope for. This one's for you. Thanks to my parents Sunniva and Bram, who read drafts, and supported me through thick and thin.

Thanks to Darren McGarvey, who inspired me to write something in this realm. To my good friend Pete Ross, who told me to get off social media and into podcasts, and acted as a valuable jargon eliminator. Thanks to my fantastic editors Mike Watson and Daniel Melo at Revol Press, without whom you wouldn't be reading this.

Thank you to my brother Sam, my sister Emma Gieben-Gamal and brother-in-law Mostafa Gamal, who cast a critical eye over early drafts. To my wonderful beta readers and advisers Tom Dove, Ewan McNichol, Ali Maloney, David-Lee Morgan, Joshua Ellis, Ewan Morrison, Catherine Grosvenor, Mark McKeown, Gary Young, Jenny Lindsay, Steve Bullivant, Graham McInnes, Bonnie Prince Bob, Iain Cameron, Yoav Segal, Douglas Gordon and Kim Betney — thank you all.

An additional hat tip to Alfie Bown of *Sublation Magazine* and Mark McGee of *You Call That Radio* for publishing my writing. An early version of the essay "Infinite Verse" was published by Sublation Magazine in 2023, and is reprinted here with permission. Thanks to the members of several secret online cabals who provided me with links to, and explanations of, everything from

Deleuze and Guattari to Dialectics; not to mention mental health resources and dank memes.

Finally, thanks to all the listeners of Strange Exiles, and all my guests on the show so far. The future's dark. Look after each other.

—Bram E. Gieben, Glasgow, 2024

Revol Press aims to revive countercultural dreaming alongside incisive materialism, emphasizing quality over 'edgy' content and hot takes, putting out considered yet incisive reflections in a timely manner. We pledge to support established writers and discover new talent, prioritizing fair royalties, ongoing dialogue, and an emphasis on quality essays and books that promote formal and theoretical innovation.

Our writers are part of a collective effort in publishing, not only making competitive royalties from their own books but taking a percentage of profits from all other books we produce and sell.

Revol is here to reassert the creative opposition of the author, in solidarity. Where once you paid lip service to the revolution and were considered credible, now you can build something revolutionary without compromise.

www.revolpress.com

Coming September 2024:

Hungry Ghosts in the Machine: Digital Capitalism and the Search for Self examines the ways in which social and other digital media utilize nostalgia to heighten anxiety, depression and alienation while offering fleeting cures which only ultimately lead to a cycle of longing and, at most, only temporary satiation. It is argued that wellbeing and spiritual practice freed of the compulsive aspect of social media use might form a useful role in a wider socialist movement. Digital era addiction, psychedelics, AI and memes meet Adorno, Deleuze, Fisher, Maté, Roderick, Sontag, Zizek, The Beatles and Metallica in Watson's characteristically cornucopian dive into the ills of 21st century living and dying.

Printed in the USA
CPSIA information can be obtained
at www.ICGtesting.com
CBHW071140010624
9377CB00018B/112